(CONTINUED FROM FRONT FLAP)

ended their weekly luncheons; how Harvard
sociologist Seymour Martin Lipset argued that
students shouldn't speak directly to faculty assemblies, because "When you admit students
the discussion, the issue naturally gravitates
their level."

It is observations like these that fill the pages
this book and explain the lost faith of today's
student generation.

# IS THE LIBRARY BURNING?

 RANDOM HOUSE • NEW YORK

# IS
# THE
# LIBRARY
# BURNING?

ROGER RAPOPORT

and

LAURENCE J. KIRSHBAUM

## DEDICATION

---

*To our parents
and Barbara*

# Author's Note

During the 1968–69 academic year we visited twenty-one university campuses* and fifteen high schools, traveling about fifty thousand miles. We interviewed hundreds of students, faculty, administrators and politicians. Convinced that the real campus troublemakers are adults, not students, we wrote this book. It is a collaboration with the exception of the prologue and the epilogue, which are signed first-person accounts.

We would like to thank the Carnegie Commission on the Future of Higher Education, its chairman Clark Kerr and his assistants Gloria Copeland and Virginia Smith. Thanks also go to Wendy Walton for typing the manuscript, Barbara Kirshbaum for her on-scene research in high schools, Ron and Joan Rapoport for numerous editorial suggestions, and Margot Lind for general aid and comfort. We are indebted to Professor William Porter of the University of Michigan, Rod Gander and James C. Jones of *Newsweek* for their years of guidance and to Bill Ganley for suggesting the title.

ROGER RAPOPORT

LAURENCF J. KIRSHBAUM

*San Francisco*
*June 10, 1969*

---

*The universities of Texas, Alabama, Michigan, Wisconsin and Chicago; the State University of New York at Buffalo, Stonybrook and Albany; the University of California at Berkeley and San Diego; San Francisco State College; Stanford; Wayne State University; Federal City College; Wisconsin State University at Oshkosh; Texas Southern University; Harvard; Cornell; Columbia; New York University and City College of New York.

# TABLE OF CONTENTS

# PROLOGUE

by

Roger Rapoport

Historians will doubtless rank April 28, 1968, as a landmark in the annals of American education, second only to passage of the Morrill Act. On that day I completed seventeen years of study, was graduated from the University of Michigan, and resigned my commission in the nation's school system. I knew education would never be the same without me, nor I the same without it. Still, I would have preferred sleeping through my own commencement as though it were one more eight-o'clock class. But my parents were flying in for the occasion. So I woke early and dashed over to the administration building to get their graduation tickets.

Inside, a secretary explained that she didn't have the

advertised tickets and directed a long line of seniors to the site of the ceremony, the domed University Events Building. While janitors obscured the basketball court with maize and blue bunting, hapless ushers ran us around the perimeter of the building to the ticket window. A uniformed guard declared, "There are no tickets left, and besides, you're not supposed to be inside this early."

In frustration I drove directly to the home of University President Robben Fleming. His wife opened the door just as the president descended the staircase with commencement speaker Robert Weaver, U.S. Secretary of Housing, who was his house guest. After being introduced to Weaver, I sat down on the living-room couch and explained the dilemma. Fleming made some unsuccessful phone calls and sent me back to the administration building. There a university administrator directed me to a ticket clerk at the Events Building who was dubious about the authenticity of my yellow plastic ID card (362–44–9616–5). I frantically flipped him my entire wallet—Social Security card, driver's license, draft card, etc.—in a final effort to get the tickets for my parents, who by now were waiting at the airport. Tickets in hand, I rushed to pick them up. We came back too late for *Pomp and Circumstance,* but soon enough to hear Weaver talk of promising career opportunities for today's graduates: "So I say to you that the urban frontier, with all of its complexities and problems, is an avenue to exciting and meaningful careers."

Afterward, we rushed off to a friend's party and pondered our glorious futures. Here amid piles of potato salad, cold cuts, and brownies was the educational elite of civilization's most advanced nation—the breast-fed generation off to conquer the world. In one corner was a comely history major who was taking her degree to the advertising department of a Boston false-teeth manufacturer. Another friend, a flaming blonde Marxist, had landed a taskless secretarial post with a New York ad agency. And I was heading for San Francisco and a free-lance writing career. But I wasn't optimistic, for I was following the path of an old friend, a sociology major who had been graduated the year before, and who was now floundering. My new roommate had been forced to supplement his writing income by serving as a guinea pig for NASA in Berkeley. He was paid twenty-five dollars a day for eating a special diet and depositing the resultant gaseous human waste into a rubber bag stuffed into the back of his pants. His gases were used to simulate the effects of astronaut exhaust fumes in the Apollo space capsule. At one point, rumor had it that an evaluation of his fumes nearly prompted the scientists to delay the entire Apollo project.

It was natural that before we embarked on our illustrious careers, our conversation drifted into anecdotes about the good old days. Finishing college is more than just completing a four-year cycle; it ends an era. Suddenly you are rid of that inner demon that has been controlling your actions since seventh grade, when an advisor waved a manilla folder at you and advised in halitosis-filled gusts: "This is C–49, your academic file where we keep records on everything you do in school. To get into college you must build a good one." I studied hard, and my teachers wrote soaring evaluations for C–49. It showed a B average, student council member, honor society member, editor of the school paper. Admission to Michigan in my senior year was automatic. So one steamy August afternoon I piled my belongings into the family Falcon, backed down the driveward and honked good-bye. I drove slowly through North Muskegon, Michigan, the town I knew so well. I sniffed the sulphurous paper mill, glanced at the foundry smoke darkening the sky, and said farewell to weedy Muskegon Lake. Soon I was on the super-highway that slices across the Michigan farmland. Three hours later I descended into the Huron River Valley, a for-ested depression in which, like a pit in a peach, nestled Ann Arbor, the technological center of the Midwest and home of the university.

I drove directly to my new residence, South Quadrangle. Built in 1954, it was a classic piece of neopenal architecture —nine stories of cinder block sheathed in red brick. The name South Quad lent proof to Marcuse's theory that words have lost all meaning. It was actually north of East Quad-rangle and adjacent to West Quadrangle (the planners gave up and named the north quadrangle Mary Markley Hall). The Quad itself contained only a patch of stubby grass; it was almost consumed by adjacent parking lots reserved for staff. I parked on a side street and lugged my suitcases up to my fourth-floor quarters, which offered a splendid view of the football stadium.

The Quad was drab but never boring. A week after I moved in, someone bombed the cafeteria. Upstairs, wrestlers rattled windows and shook walls during their nocturnal practice. After lighted cigarette butts incinerated our mail-box, the postmaster put up a warning notice, which was promptly burned down. The dim, brown corridors were enlivened by jars of urine splashed under doors, heads jok-ingly stuffed in flushing toilets, boxes of manure placed on elevators, and buturic acid poured into ventilators. Maids opened doors to find naked rear ends mooning at them.

Amid all this horseplay, the silver-haired president was kind enough to remind us at our opening convocation that we were "the most talented freshman class in the history of the university." Stressing the quality control that had gone into the selection of our class, he gestured madly, like Moses parting the Red Sea, and summoned wave upon wave of my fellow students to their feet—first the high school valedictorians, then the salutatorians, finally the student body presidents.

Orientation week followed. First we learned how to find the health service and get football tickets. Then came a battery of placement tests. I was particularly nervous about the French test (in high school my teacher had passed me on the promise that I would never reveal she had been my instructor). I almost flunked the oral part of the placement exam, which was read by a professor from Japan with an unusual French accent. Next came psychological testing with true-false questions such as, "I prefer eating raw carrots to cooked carrots." (The test presumed a correlation between personal preference and career motivation.) These results were slipped into a folder with my high school record, which I took to Angell Hall auditorium. My counselor was one of twenty conferring in the auditorium. He had the third aisle. I sat down beside him and we shook hands. It took him a mere five minutes to sign me up for history and political science (which I didn't want but needed for a social science requirement), journalism (which I didn't want but needed for a sequence), and French (which I simply didn't want). As he handed over my course card, I tried to protest. But he simply smiled. "Don't worry, you've got to take 120 credit hours in four years, and that's a lot of hours."

Next was registration. To some of us the procedures that followed seemed like what we had read about Nazi concentration camps. We were herded into the basement of

Victoria Waterman Gymnasium in small groups. Our pictures were shot in the basement weight room. In the wrestling room student clerks handed out our IBM cards and steered us to the locker room, temporarily filled with fencing to form a maze. At a checkpoint, student guards stamped and sorted our papers. Panic swept the lines when we saw that the shower room was our next stop. It turned out to be a tuition check for in-state students, who pay lower fees. After passing under the harmless nozzles, we were guided up a stairway to sign up for "psychological experiments." Upstairs we paid tuition, made last-minute adjustments on courses, and then dribbled off the basketball court with smudged carbon "class schedules" to tack up on the dorm bulletin board.

Although I didn't know who my new teachers were, I figured they would certainly beat my high school instructors, like the one in world history who ran dry halfway through the period and turned on a radio for the Paul Harvey midday news. But I soon discovered my college professors didn't have much to say either. In Political Science 101, sixteen dull lectures led to a midterm examination asking, "Briefly compare the origins, theory and practice of Communism and Democracy." Small discussion classes weren't much better, just harder to sleep in. Under orders from the top of the departmental hierarchies, teaching fellows taught us as though we were retarded. In French we got a bowdlerized version of *Candide* and a timecard to punch three hours a week at the language laboratory, where a technician just in from Argentina feebly tried to give aid in Spanish. In English composition we had to write 1,500 words on "How to Make a Succulent Hamburger." There was little reassurance when I discovered a copy of the departmental manual, which advised the teaching fellows, "Socially, the teacher has to recognize that the students in his section, however inept their prose and surly their manner, are basically reasonable human beings."

In order to fulfill the natural science sequences, I elected astronomy. Class turned out to be a varsity-club meeting. All the athletes sat like a *Playboy* all-American team draped across the front row. "The Doc," as we knew her, was a short, elderly woman passionately devoted to the Wolverines. She even dressed like a cheerleader, in saddle shoes, bobby socks, bulky sweater, and pleated skirt. Her grading system was rumored to be A for athlete, B for boy, and C for coed. This was an exaggeration, of course, but athletes seldom floundered.

All the Doc's tests were based on old exams. When midterms came along, every Xerox machine in town hummed. The "jock" fraternity houses kept up their files of old exams as faithfully as they polished their trophies. At finals time, athletes facing grade-point trouble would come to her home —a kind of local hall of fame—and offer her trinkets (team watches, fraternity pins, autographed balls) to add to her glittering collection. In return she might slip them a few clues on the exam questions. During my freshman year, Michigan went to the Rose Bowl. The Doc was so excited that she didn't bother to turn in semester grades by the Christmas deadline. The registrar tracked her down in California, but she stood her ground. "Fire me if you don't like it," she told them from Pasadena.

Sometime during my first year, I realized the biggest headache was not "depersonalization" but "overpersonalization." If you leave them alone, 30,000 students can probably coexist happily with each other. But like any bureaucracy, a large university has too many of the wrong kind of people in the wrong place. One example was the "resident advisor," a bitter graduate student with a powerful antenna for marijuana, who lived on my corridor. The dorm "housemother," who also lived on my floor in a corner suite, was another pest. It was rumored that she had once dated a young Army officer named Dwight Eisenhower. But now she was just a nasty hen muttering like a psychology instructor about "anxiety" and "deviance" and "Spock babies" whenever an ashtray was missing from the lounge.

Privacy didn't exist, and we had no place to go. Girls were sequestered on the other side of the dorm and only allowed in our rooms for three hours a month during "open-opens"—provided three legs were kept on the floor. Under the dorm rules at that time, a girl coming in five minutes after curfew was penalized; a girl who stayed out all night would not be punished. The girls often circumvented this nonsense by dating older boys with apartments. Those freshmen with steady girls resorted to cars, music rooms, church basements. However, some had to use dorm lounges. One couple, a disheveled pair whom we called "Cyclone and Flopsy," used to have a nightly encounter on a high-backed sofa in a main floor lounge. I'd be reading and suddenly notice a crescent shape rising above the sofa and then disappearing behind the back.

■

Despite the setbacks in the dorm and the classroom, I never would have comprehended the total frustration of college without the four-story undergraduate library, a sterile, glass-enclosed cage fronted by a gravel-pit lawn. The UGLI, as it was called, was more lonely-hearts club than library. Girls flocked there to distract boys from their studies. The sorority girls, who gathered in the fourth-floor art-print gallery, were a typical diversion. They were checking out Reubens, Giotto, and Brueghel; all I could see was Odalisque lying there waiting for me. Downstairs wasn't much better. My concentration was broken by the creaking chairs and clacking typewriters, the whirring library computer and vulturous cleaning ladies slamming down ashtrays. I usually ended up at a table, looking out at the revolving Ann Arbor Bank sign down the block. The electric lights enumerated my failure: 7:30 and 20° (page 1), 8:02 and 15° (page 8), 10:35 and 12° (page 22).

Because it was impossible to study efficiently, I would end up in the UGLI seven days a week. By Sunday night, after eight straight hours, the world would be closing in on me. Exhausted and depressed, I would try to clear my head by going outside and standing in the chill wind. I would peer through the glass and see, amid the bubbly lights inside, thousands of students bent over their books, each like Boris Karloff over a test tube.

One Sunday something snapped inside me. I had been studying an astronomy problem and got hung-up on a logarithim. I couldn't begin to do the assignment, so finally I just crossed out my name on the front of the book, shut it, and left it on the table, where the cleaning woman would nosily swoop it up.

After freshman year I moved out of the dorm into a neighborhood of old, cluttered houses and dilapidated apartments. The Quad experience gives shape to my memory of freshman year. The remaining three years were a blur. College never led me on to anything; I felt the same as a senior as I did when I was a sophomore. The days were indistinguishable. I spent nights on couches while roommates and girlfriends took the bedroom. In the mornings I rose, stretched to the ceiling, and a piece of acoustical tile would pop out. I ate Lifesavers for breakfast, went back to bed for a "noonsie" at lunchtime, and then feasted on hamburgers at dinner. I opened a can of lard, flipped a glob into the skillet, and then threw in a half pound of frozen ground beef from the freezer. As the hamburger thawed in the bubbling lard, I gradually sliced off melting chunks and formed them into a patty that finally crumbled into a greasy Sloppy Joe. Afterward I threw the dishes into the three-day-old puddle in the sink and headed for the language lab, which was closed. So I came back, conjugated French, watched Johnny Carson, and fell asleep again on the couch.

The days rolled weirdly by, and then suddenly I slammed smack into the examination period. I can remember the feeling at 2 A.M. when the snow was falling outside, and only six hours remained before a final exam. I'd put aside lists of key facts, thinking back on those early-semester resolutions. Like all courses, this one had begun well. The professor had an international reputation and an exciting reading list. But somewhere it all fell apart. The books proved to be scholarly treatises only an author's mother could finish. The first-day jokes gave way to disorganized soliloquies. I wanted to assimilate material, fitting facts into concepts. The professors wanted over-all knowledge accumulation as told to a computer via multiple-choice tests. So at the end of the semester I was not pulling together what I had learned; I was taking it apart. I broke down all the concepts into isolated facts, dates, treaties, and names—the stuff that grades are made of. In the morning my class met for the exam. The professor handed out mimeographed questions. When I had filled in all the computer blocks, I turned in the answer sheet (silently, so as not to disturb those still working). Then I went home for vacation to recuperate. Two weeks later a postcard arrived from the professor. No inscription, not even a signature, just a scrawl: "Political Science 401, Grade: C."

As I talked with older, graduating friends, it became clear that I had to unpin my hopes from the university classroom. To think of going on to graduate school meant being professionalized into an academic automaton. A friend in dentistry was forced to shave his modest sideburns lest they "pick up infectious bacteria from the spray of the high-speed drill." Unless I was going to become an academic, a lawyer, a CPA, or some other carefully defined careerist, school was a liability.

So, as early as my freshman year, I began to treat college as a part-time job. By no means was I a drop-out; I still took my courses and passed. But like my friends, I shifted my commitment outside the classroom. There were a variety of alternatives, such as SDS and student government. As an aspiring writer I chose the campus paper, the *Michigan Daily*. No prerequisites were required for admission to the *Daily*. There were no examinations or term papers. The hours were ideal, noon to 2 A.M. A clattering AP machine kept the *Daily* up to date, while radical students and staffers engaged in endless discussions in which I found the intimacy and intellectualism lacking in the classroom. The paper was not bogged down in the academic seniority system. While still a freshman I was sent to Selma, Alabama, to cover the civil rights demonstrations and wrote numerous signed editorials on how to better mankind.

Outraged administrators accused *Daily* writers and radicals of naiveté. I always felt the *Daily*'s most powerful weapon was its ability to unite the journalist's nose and the child's eye, a devastating combination when applied to the stench and confusion of corporate university management. My own awakening came while following a tip about one of the most powerful regents, Eugene Power, who ran a microfilm company with a parasitic relationship to the university library. Power's firm, University Microfilms, was in the business of converting 5,000 "borrowed" books a week into saleable microfilm copies— without paying royalties. In addition, two special microfilm cameras had been installed in the UGLI to copy rare books, some of which would disappear off the shelves for six months. When I asked the library director why Power's firm wasn't at least paying a fine for overdue materials, he didn't appreciate it. Regent Power himself stalled on an appointment for three weeks. Finally, flanked by obsequious aides, he sat down with me. He shed little light on his business affairs, ushered me out like a rebellious servant, and admonished, "Behave yourself, son." My story ran, despite a plea by the library director's physician that his coronary patient would suffer a fatal heart attack. A subsequent attorney general's investigation found Power in conflict of interest. He resigned his post.

The other regents were no improvement. They were absentee landlords who visited their property two days a month. Their ephemeral presence was the clue that the university was not run by its constituents, but by corporate ambassadors. Chauffered limousines swept them off campus to deliberations in a baroque mansion graced with tranquil oaks, rolling lawns, reflecting pools, and a panoramic view of the Huron River Valley. The deliberations normally began on Thursday. All decisions had to be completed by noon Friday in order to give the news service time to prepare press releases in advance of the formal 2 P.M. "public meeting."

I always suspected that the regents met in private lest their personal idiosyncrasies be exposed. One intimate session took place in a suite at the Ponchartrain Hotel, where they were wooing a new president, Robben Fleming. Since Fleming is a teetotaler, the cocktails consisted of sherry. But one regent, unable to contain himself, would periodically disappear into the bathroom where he had hidden a flask under a towel.

The public meetings, required by constitutional statute, were equally ridiculous. The vice-presidents offered faithful little soliloquies while the sleepier regents dozed behind sunglasses. "A new French house is going into the Oxford Housing Unit," declared the vice-president for student affairs. Will there be French plumbing?" inquired a regent, convulsing his colleagues.

At first, many students thought they could crack this anachronistic structure with the help of liberal administrative allies. It seemed logical that a bright young administrator could work from within to subvert the system for the benefit of the students. Accordingly, student radicals worked hard to put a popular liberal psychology professor in office as vice-president for student affairs. On taking office he promised to be a "vice-president presenting the student interest to the regents and the president." But we soon learned otherwise.

When the House Un-American Activities Committee subpoenaed sixty-five students and faculty members belonging to radical groups, he gave in, and withheld announcement of the decision until after the *Daily* had suspended publication for the summer. He refused to honor a campus referendum that had gone two-to-one against the university's practice of ranking students for the draft. Then he tried to ban sit-ins and finally wound up making secret attempts to discipline

SDS leaders for antiwar protests.

Naturally he was showered with abuse for having "sold out." But rather than trying to explain himself to students (he was, after all, still vice-president), he withdrew into his somber Danish-modern office and brooded. The *Daily* reporters were denied interviews. Radicals noticed that he had even drawn the shades and locked his door to thwart imaginary sit-ins. Eventually he became tired of his role and quit, only to be rewarded by an appointment as special advisor on urban problems.

Like adults everywhere, he wanted students to reinforce his own expectations, confirm what his generation had done, and stabilize his life's work. At heart, the campus administrators were only subtler versions of the forty-two-year-old Ann Arbor police lieutenant who arrested campus cinema leaders for showing suggestive underground movies. His critical review seemed to be based more on fear than artistic judgment. "The students are going down the same path that caused the Roman Empire to fall," he explained. "When laws break down, that promotes anarchy which leads to dictatorship. Now think what that could do to a man like me. Say I'm in my twenty-fourth year on the police force here and looking forward to my retirement pension after twenty-five years service. Some dictator could come and cancel that plan and I'd be out of luck. That's why, when you have a good system, you have to support it."

But I hadn't signed up for any pension plan yet. Unlike the lieutenant, I was not committed to perpetuation of the Ann Arbor police. Unlike the administration, I was not committed to perpetuation of the university in its present form. I saw that obedience to the school system required people to forget about each other. One had to get out of school to be human, for taking school seriously meant wrapping oneself up in a meaningless schedule that did not allow time to know or talk to others. It meant teachers knew their students better by their handwriting than their faces. It meant students had to war with each other needlessly on the grade-point battle-field. It meant locked offices and silent libraries to preclude conversation. College cut people off instead of bringing them together.

I recall running into a favorite poetry teacher once when I was pulling out of the Thompson Street parking ramp at the end of a hectic day. For the past few weeks I had been unsuccessfully trying to fit into his tight schedule. But now we had our chance. We talked hurriedly through my car window until impatient drivers honked me out of the six-story structure. As I drove into the night air, and he walked the concrete maze to his car, I thought about the great truths we might have exchanged at that same moment in another situation. Freed from our respective roles, all of us, teacher, student, and administrator, could have learned from each other. But bogged down in the endless academic bureaucracy, we had no time for one another.

Still, I tried to reassure myself from time to time, only to have the truth thrown back at me. I remember the night I spent cramming with a friend for my last set of finals. Lying dazed on a couch, amid study guides, Xeroxed notes, and dog-eared old exams, I mused, "It's tough now. But I'll bet twenty-five years from now we'll look back on these as the best years of our lives." My friend, wrestling with incompletes, a late paper, and the final, grimaced and said, "Go ahead and think that if it makes you feel good. But my memory is better than that."

Somber thoughts for a graduation party; but they were

honest ones. When it was all over, I took my parents back to the airport and devoted my last evening in Ann Arbor to packing. In the basement I found forgotten piles of note-books, paperbacks, love letters, and exams. My ash cans filled quickly, so at midnight I quietly piled the overflow into my neighbor's back yard. The next morning I took a cab to the airport. On the way out of town, I made one last sentimental stop. The driver pulled up in front of the UGLI, and I raced inside to pay a $3.25 library fine that was blocking my diploma. Now I was free.

# CHAPTER 1:

# ANATOMY OF A RIOT

Oshkosh, Wisconsin, is the kind of town SNCC leader H. Rap Brown had in mind when he called "violence . . . as American as cherry pie." The town's brawling image dates back to its nineteenth century heyday as a Midwestern, sawmill citadel where brawny loggers lived off Chief Oshkosh Beer. For over a hundred years the phrase "Having Fun with the Boys in Oshkosh" has been synonymous with violence.[1] Oshkosh's

[1]The phrase originated in a classic tall tale "Going to Oshkosh to Have A Little Fun With the Boys," first published in 1866 in the Fond du Lac *Commonwealth*. It was reprinted world-wide and plagued Oshkoshians for years. It went as follows:

"We have recently heard a good story—good only as it represents the moral condition of Oshkosh society. A minister from a neighboring town

frontier reputation even prompted the *New York Times* to caution tourists in 1877: "No Eastern man has visited Oshkosh and returned again to civilization. One determined Massachusetts man set out upon a journey in search of Oshkosh . . . penetrated as far as Waukegan . . . and vanished into the wilderness."

---

started to go over there one day last week on a sort of missionary enterprise. He drove his own team and when within six miles of the end of his journey met a man limping along, with blood running down one side of his face. The minister asked him if that was the road to Oshkosh.

'Yes, you are on the right road. I just came from there; I've been up there having a little fun with the boys.'

About two miles further he met another man, one arm in a sling, one eye badly bunged, and his clothing in a badly delapidated condition.

'How far is it to Oshkosh?' asked the minister.

'Only (h-i-c) five miles,' answered the pitiable object. 'Oshkosh is a live town; I've just been up there having a little fun with the boys.'

With a sad heart the minister drove on, falling into a reverie on the depravity of man in general and the Oshkoshians in particular, when he suddenly came upon a man sitting by the side of the road. One leg was sprained, one ear had been bitten off, and seated by a puddle of water, he was seeking relief by bathing the parts affected. The minister was awestruck. Stopping his horse, he asked the man what terrible accident had befallen him.

'Oh, not any at all,' responded the bleeding wretch. 'I have only been up to Oshkosh, having a little fun with the boys.'

'I suppose you mean by that that you have been engaged in a brutal fight,' said the minister.

'Yes,' answered the man, 'I have heard that is what they call it down at Fond du Lac, but they don't call it by that name up at Oshkosh; there they call it having a little fun with the boys.'

'What do you suppose your wife will say when she sees you?' asked the reverend gentleman.

At this the man looked up with a sardonic smile. Putting his hand in his pocket, he pulled out a piece of nose, a large lock of hair to which a part of the scalp was attached, and a piece of flesh which he had bitten from the cheek of his opponent, and holding them up for the minister's inspection growled out, 'There, what do you suppose his wife will say when she sees him?'

This was a squelcher. As anxious as the minister was to do good, he was not prepared to invade the devil's stronghold, and turning around he returned home. The next time he starts on a missionary enterprise to the frontier town of Oshkosh he will take good care not to go alone. He likes a little fun now and then, but he doesn't care about having it 'with the boys.'"

But the twentieth century brought a veneer of civilization to the Fox River Valley citadel of 53,000. Oshkosh B'Gosh Co., a widely known overall-maker, diversified into the sportswear field. The Leach Co. built there the world's most modern garbage truck plant. Meanwhile the city began hosting the "Miss Wisconsin" pageant and won national awards for its pedestrian safety program. Still, Oshkosh was not fully civilized until mid-century, when its obscure teachers' college blossomed into Oshkosh State University.

The campus, virtually hidden in an old residential neighborhood, had lain fallow for decades. Only four new buildings were built between 1871 and the mid-1950s. The enrollment in 1955 was a paltry 1,164. But then the State University master plan designated Oshkosh for cultivation into a "comprehensive university with 18,000 students by 1975." Since the school had "been without an 'academic specialty' for 40 years," the report saw Oshkosh as the natural place to build a "broad base of (new) academic majors and departments. . . . Expanding WSU-O is mandatory if Wisconsin is to retain its competitive position in national markets."

To turn these proposals into reality, the state hired master planner Roger E. Guiles to take over the Oshkosh presidency in 1959. An architect of the Wisconsin higher-educaton plan, Guiles had a strong background in high school and college administration. Under his leadership builders transformed the campus landscape by adding thirty new buildings, including Clow Social Science Center, Halsey Science Center, Reeve Union, even a planetarium. An elevator ride to the tenth floor of shiny, new Gruenhagen Hall opened up a view all the way to Fond Du Lac. In Guiles' first decade as president, he increased enrollment from 2,000 to 12,000. From his office on the second floor of Dempsey

Hall, tall, steely Guiles presided over the campus like a high-school principal. He suspended rambunctious undergraduates for participating in snowball fights. His vice-president for academic affairs, E. O. Thedinga, personally patrolled the corridors peering in classroom windows to make sure teachers were meeting their classes.

Parents were proud to stick the Oshkosh State decal on the family station wagon. When a TV announcer intoned, "It's eleven o'clock, do you know where your children are?" mothers knew their daughters were locked into the dormitory because of the weeknight curfew, and not running wild like those roving hippie bands in Madison. Fathers knew their sons would be worrying about ornate ice sculpture and home-coming floats instead of Fanon and Che. An Oshkosh parent could pick up the phone without fearing his child would be on the other end of the line pleading for bail money.

However, Oshkosh was still a long way from being the "first-level university" envisioned by the master planners. Many students were lured by Oshkosh's low admission standards; state residents in the upper three-fourths of their high-school class were automatically accepted. Teachers complained that many of the students spent more time in off-campus bars than in the classroom. Even political activism flickered briefly, when the state legislature contemplated raising the drinking age from eighteen to twenty one. Students staged a "beer riot" and marched all the way to Highway 41. President Guiles put the ringleaders on probation.

At the same time, Guiles was having trouble implementing the master plan, which called for expansion of the liberal arts curriculum and teacher education, a new graduate division, and four new professional schools. The State Coordinating Council stalled necessary accreditation for new departments and degree programs. Anthropology teachers, hired to set up a new department, left in 1969 when the coordinating council witheld sanction. Soaring enrollment also gave faculty a heavy twelve-hour course-load, making each responsible for up to 450 students. Without teaching assistants to serve as graders, exams frequently had to be computerized. Economy measures included deferring the second semester of freshman composition to the junior year, when normal academic attrition cut enrollment by nearly 50 percent. Additional problems occurred when Faculty Senate Chairman Robert Field let "One girl pursue a German degree on the presumption that the coordinating council would authorize us to offer a German major. Final approval for the major didn't come through until a month before she graduated. It was a close call." Field also found an added hassle in "getting used to thinking in terms of what the computer needs. There were a lot of new forms we had to learn how to fill out."

Nonetheless, the growth at Oshkosh offered exciting new challenges. According to the plan, the "student-centered university" featured "dormitories where democratic interaction" allowed "students from rural areas, Milwaukee suburbs, Negro core areas and business communities to mingle, interact, and develop understanding, respect for human dignity, tolerance, and respect for the dissenter." All this meant that Oshkosh needed more than just white students. So under Guiles' leadership, Oshkosh State recruiters began moving eastward during 1964. Among the dark denizens of Milwaukee, 80 miles to the southeast the recruiters lived off native soul food while tempting blacks to come to school in all-white Winnebagoland. At largely black high schools, such as Milwaukee North, Lincoln and Riverside, the recruiters explained the unique opportunities at Oshkosh. Black enrollment jumped to 114 by 1968. Typically, black Milwaukee applicants such as Jeff McCreary saw Oshkosh as the sensible compromise between leading state schools. Madison was too tough academically; Platteville and Whitewater were too small. Oshkosh was perfect.

The master plan called for "developing a special program for the culturally disadvantaged." This would include extra counseling, tutorials, modification of curriculums, and "programs to make local students, faculty and townspeople more knowledgeable of the history, culture, and problems of the disadvantaged students." President Guiles entrusted the black students to the remarkably-named Advisory Committee for Culturally Distinct Students. However, the busy president stayed out of direct dealings with blacks. He explained: "In general I don't have much direct contact with students so I would have no reason to have contact with black students. That's not the function of this office."

Guiles was perfectly willing to brag about the program off campus. On November 21, 1968, he was planning to drive to Madison and take his place as panelist at a statewide conference on aid to black students. He intended to tell an audience of 200 top Wisconsin educators about Oshkosh's success in importing new black talent. But the veteran educator didn't make the conference. Stopping by the office at 8:30 A.M. to pick up his conference notes, Guiles noticed a strange sight. There were black students, over ninety of them, standing at the door. President Guiles asked the group of unfamiliar faces if they had an appointment. The blacks didn't reply, but silently filed into his office without bothering to introduce themselves. They demanded that Guiles immediately accept a list of four demands: more black courses, more black teachers, establishment of an Afro-American cultural center, and the firing of a white director of financial aids.

A month earlier, working through his Advisory Committee for Culturally Distinct Students, Guiles had agreed to only the first three demands. But after the administration offered the old journalism house for the cultural-center facility, the blacks discovered it was scheduled for demolition the following summer. Also, the hiring of black teachers and the setting-up of new black curriculums was moving slowly.

Guiles again reviewed the students' list of demands. This time he expressed a fear that the cultural center would become a segregated citadel for black revolutionaries. Apparently the president had not understood the month-old proposal for an integrated cultural center aimed at exposing white Oshkosh to black art, literature, music, and history. Disgusted, one of the blacks yelled, "Do your thing!" and some of the students proceeded to damage several thousand dollars worth of executive office-equipment. "Don't hurt anyone and don't take any money—anything else goes," shouted one of the students as typewriters, desks, file cabinets, and drapes were thrown to the floor. The blacks finished their work in ten minutes and walked out. Vice-president for development Sherman E. Gunderson, moaned "It will take an experienced secretary three weeks to put the files back in order."

Ninety-four blacks and four whites came back an hour later and staged a sit-in at Dempsey Hall. Local police moved in, rounded up the group into rental vans and took them off to jail. The town of Oshkosh was outraged. "There are those who say these troublemakers should be out of town by sundown," thundered the afternoon edition of the *Oshkosh Daily*

*Northwestern.* After the 94 blacks and four whites were released from the county jail on a $250 bond each, Guiles
waited one day to suspend them. Then he closed the school
and sent the entire campus home for an early Thanksgiving
recess. News of the event circled the globe. Oshkosh was
no longer a vaudeville joke.

The riot stands as a valuable primer to the student power
movement. Thanks to Guiles, the conservative Midwestern
college had had no tradition of campus activism, and none of
the New Left prophets or faculty radicals credited with man-
ufacturing revolt on more-publicized campuses. The night
before the fateful protest, editors of Oshkosh's campus paper,
the *Advance Titan,* had stayed up to finish off a gala, four-
color homecoming souvenir edition. When they awoke the
next morning, the editors were dumbfounded. The public
was equally confused. Hadn't the blacks been getting what
they wanted? Townspeople were flabbergasted at the uproar
over the black curriculum. As one Oshkosh resident told a
WOSH-AM talk show, "Why do we need courses in black
history? You can study that overnight." Oshkosh politicians
like State Assemblyman Jack D. Steinhelber couldn't see
what led the blacks to tearing up the president's office. "Sure
there's racism in Oshkosh, but no more than in Milwaukee
or Madison. They are biting the hand that feeds them. Anyone that would do that doesn't belong in this institution. They
have set their case back a hundred years."

The administration succeeded in banishing the blacks,
but not the ills that prompted the revolt. As Oshkosh political
science professor David Roth explained, "Those black kids
were reflecting the pent-up frustration of a lot of us around
here. They did the dirty work for us."

In many ways the program for the "culturally distinct"

was doomed from the start. Black freshman Theopolis Williams was a case in point. When he stepped off the train from Milwaukee in January 1966, icy blasts were sweeping in off Lake Winnebago. It was 27° below zero. The seventeen-year-old sped to campus and found no Welcome Wagon out to greet him the first day. After a hard search he turned up an African, one of the eight other black men on campus. The town itself was even less inviting. For a black, the streets of Oshkosh were like frontier Abilene, Kansas. In bars (the only entertainment), he was pierced by white hate-stares and taunted for his negritude. Williams quickly discovered that the shouts of "nigger" were more than threats. Bands of white toughs were out for blood, so he took a cue from his black brothers and carried weapons— a Japanese hari-kari knife hooked to his right leg and a razor in his back pocket. No black man dared walk the streets alone at night. Says Williams, "We kept in top shape, fighting condition. For self-protection we stuck together just like a little army. We went to class together, showered together, ate together, and met at certain times in the Union."

Fortunately, reinforcements were on the way. In fall, 1967, sixty-five blacks enrolled. Says Williams, "The white hoods were getting scared because there were so many of us. They wanted to chase us out of town." That prompted the big showdown at the Titan Tavern, a favorite off-campus bar. The blacks were badly outnumbered. The rumble began when a white youth shoved black student Russell Jones away from the tavern jukebox as his white comrades shouted epithets. Then the white gang's leader arrived, stripped down to his T-shirt, flexed his muscles, and elicited a war whoop from his followers. Williams recalls, "They looked at us and said, 'Oh, all you black men better leave now, or you gonna get killed.' We went up to their leader and told them, 'Step outside and the shit is on.' So while they were doing all this foolish primping and showing off, we ran outside and got bricks and boards together. When the twenty-six of them came out, the ten of us whipped their ass. After it was over, we wasn't even scratched. The next time they saw us they gave us all the respect in the world. They had to learn the hard way."

But the blacks still didn't feel at home in Oshkosh. In class they were treated like a sideshow. Gerald Thomas of Newark, New Jersey, remembers: "White kids kept coming up to me and telling me they had never seen a black person before coming to Oshkosh." One teacher made an informal poll of her seminar and found that eighteen out of forty students had encountered their first black person in Oshkosh. The blacks found white social life sterile. On campus, the fraternities and sororities monopolized extracurricular life with noisy parties, carnivals, and homecoming competitions. The blacks were excluded from the Greek groups. Off campus, social life centered around the bars. But as Jerry Benston of Milwaukee put it, "I didn't come to college to drink beer, listen to psychedelic music, and play pinball machines. I can do that at home." Lonely, the blacks often deserted their bleak Oshkosh dormitories for Milwaukee on the weekends.

On Mondays they would return to courses that always seemed to skip the appropriate references to black persons. Like the whites, black students also protested the pettiness of the grading system, which allowed teachers to arbitrarily mark down for such things as excessive footnoting on a term paper. When Theopolis Williams complained about grades, his instructors would explain, "Mr. Williams, I'm the teacher and you're the student." Finally he exploded when a teacher gave him a C on a carefully written, thirty-two-page history paper. "If you won't give me at least a B on this paper, you won't be in this university any more, because I'm going to take it to the department chairman, the dean, and even the president until I get the right mark." Two weeks later the teacher called Williams back, said she had reread the paper and the best she could give him was an A minus. Unfortunately these tactics did little good for the over-all black grade-point average, which stood at 1.3 (D) in fall, 1967, compared with the all-campus C average. Black attrition was double that of white. Over two-thirds of the black freshmen didn't even make it to sophomore year.

Those who did manage to pass became increasingly fed up with campus life. "All I'm getting here is four years of whiteness. They're trying to program me into a white man," complained Jerry Benston. Pretty sophomore Sandra McCreary lamented that she didn't feel at home. "I come from a place [Milwaukee] where I am not afraid to go out at night, but in Oshkosh I go with four or five other students. . . . When I go into an Oshkosh department store I am stared at. . . . I have been called 'nigger' when I walk down the streets of Oshkosh. And I don't want to be the underdog any longer." Of course the administration sympathized with some of these problems. As Registrar Donald Jorgenson saw it, "There was a haircutting incident, some charges of discrimination in off-campus housing, a few cases of verbal obscenities, and a more general feeling of being stared at—the usual treatment that unfortunately blacks find in white America." Worried, the administration tried to head off black unrest through an integrated civil rights group under university jurisdiction. Financial support was even lined up through the community.

But the token group floundered, and in spring, 1968, seven militants started a black student union. Recruiting moved slowly at first. "You're crazy to start a BSU in Oshkosh, you'll get yourself killed," potential black members told organizer Theopolis Williams. But the founders propagandized effectively and enlisted nearly all the sixty-five black students in town. By-laws were set up that excluded white members.

Soon the blacks were politicking for the first BSU president. The women fell behind bearded Mike Gordon of New York, and the men backed Russell Jones of Milwaukee. Gordon was elected president by one vote at a stormy meeting in April, 1968. But Jones leaped to the front of the group and declared, "I'm not going to stand this shit. I'm going to be president, and anyone who wants to try to replace me is going to have to kick my ass." The girls screamed for Gordon, but he declined the post out of in fear. Jones was inaugurated under the watchful eyes of the black men.

By the fall of 1968, a nervous Oshkosh administration was rushing to head off the militants. Registrar Donald Jorgenson started to realize that the school had not prepared adequately for the blacks. "We should have had a budget to finance special black courses, speakers and programs before we brought these kids up. You can't bring black students in and not be ready for them. Our intentions were good but we just didn't know what we were doing." To remedy the situation, the administration hired twenty-eight-year-old James McKee, a Michigan State University graduate student, to become 'Director of Programs for Culturally Distinct Groups." The first American Negro to become a faculty member in Oshkosh history, McKee quickly found that fights, discrimination, and academic hang-ups "had prompted an incredible drop-out rate among black students. Only three blacks had actually graduated from Oshkosh." McKee's assistant turned out to be the third black graduate, twenty-three-year-old Philip Layne.

McKee soon found he was a fireman without a truck. Shoved into a Dempsey Hall office, the black newcomer discovered that he had "no budget, no power and no secretarial staff outside a part-time student employee who came in when she had a free moment. I could take a trip but as far as changing the university or hiring someone, I was at a loss. The administration just brought me in to get to know the black students by their first names so I could go over to a black demonstration and say, 'Now Johnny, you know you shouldn't be doing this picketing here.' And then Johnny was supposed to reply, 'Yes sir, rightaway, boss. I'll go back to my dorm and study.' "

McKee also soon discovered that the campus bureaucracy shuffled all black students his way. "If a black kid had a problem the attitude was 'Send him to Mr. McKee.' So kids came to see me about their chemistry homework. Hell, I don't know anything about chemistry." Twenty-eight-year-old Justin Obi, a Nigerian-born chemistry instructor, volunteered to aid black students when he joined the staff in the fall of 1968. He was rebuffed. "The administration told me that first-year instructors like myself were not allowed to counsel students." Like the black students, Obi found racial trouble at Oshkosh. His white wife was snubbed by the chemistry department chairman at cocktail parties.

Increasingly fed up with radical and academic troubles, the blacks withdrew into closed BSU meetings. Black administrator McKee was shut out, although the students used him as an intermediary. "The BSU let me know what they thought I should be doing. On October 15, they presented a list of demands which I took to the campus Committee on the Culturally Distinct. . . ." With the blessing of President Guiles, the committee informed the students on October 25 that their demands for increased black curriculum and faculty and for an Afro-American study center would be met. The center was the key demand. The blacks felt this was the best way for them to win recognition as something more than fishermen who came up from Milwaukee each summer to troll Lake Winnebago.

But implementation moved slowly. On the night of November 20, the group met for three hours and decided to cut red tape by confronting Guiles. After the smash-in, and the arrests and suspensions that followed, there was further hassling in court. The blacks filed an affidavit of prejudice against their Winnebago Country Court Judge James V. Sitter, who had remarked to two mumbling young defendants earlier in the year, "Speak up, boys, you're talking like niggers." President Guiles defended Sitter by explaining, "It wasn't a racist remark, the judge only meant nigger in the sense of illiteracy." Judge Sitter added in self-defense that his "daughter talks that way all the time," but eventually he transferred jurisdiction of the case to the State Circuit Court. In March, ninety-one former black students pleaded guilty on unlawful assembly charges and were fined $125.

The protest took its toll on campus. Professors such as chemist Justin Obi, who protested the suspensions, were not rehired for the coming year. Others, such as Professor Janet Feagans, who had spoken out for the blacks, were flooded with hate mail. One high school teacher chastised Miss Feagans for backing the blacks, who "had probably been driven up from Milwaukee in their father's Cadillacs and Continentals." Disgusted by this climate, dozens of teachers resolved to leave. Departing Political Science Chairman George Willis ran a placement service for twelve of his fourteen professors seeking new jobs. In January futile efforts were made to get the blacks reinstated. Student sympathizers planted black crosses on the lawn in front of Dempsey Hall to honor the exiled students. They were burned down by vandals. About 40 percent of the suspended students enrolled in other colleges (although Madison and several other schools refused to accept them). The rest took jobs or were drafted. The administration denied requests for reinstatement until the summer of 1969, explaining that the suspension "could be considered quite moderate. . . . The Board (of Regents) did not expel, they only suspended. The length of the suspension was only one full semester. It could hardly have been less because that would have been less than the suspension that is provided for academic failure."

However, suspending the blacks did not end activism in Oshkosh. In the spring the administration was keeping its eye on new radical weeds springing up around campus. SDS, draft-resistance and peace-forum strength were growing. A well-edited underground paper was being widely circulated for the first time. Even over at Oshkosh High School a new radical movement was building momentum. But for the moment, Oshkosh State was back in business as the largest producer of teachers in Wisconsin.

# CHAPTER 2:

# THE FACULTY

As he does every morning at 8 A.M., Associate Professor of Sociology Gerald Marwell, 32, drops his son off at nursery school on his walk to the office. But this Monday, February 10, 1969, is not a normal day for Marwell or his 2,000 faculty colleagues at the University of Wisconsin in Madison. The students have called a strike to support their thirteen demands built around an "autonomous" black studies department. During the next twenty-four hours, Marwell is like a latter-day Leopold Bloom on an incongruent odyssey through disrupted classes, special faculty meetings, even the "Laugh-In" for comic relief. Finally, at dawn, he journeys to nighttown, in this case the departmental office, where he tenderly monitors a sit-in while grading a thesis.

Marwell has left a diary of this day that is a documentary of the faculty member under stress. It reveals that like any professional man, he cannot view his own life with scientific detachment. His general sympathy for the students is under-cut by a raw instinct — the urge for self-preservation. A creature of habit, Marwell's first reaction to the strike at 8:30 A.M. is to fish the list of thirteen demands from atop his cluttered desk and rewrite its oblique English. It is therefore no accident that he can view the strike only in his own terms.

At a special noon departmental meeting, where a group of sociology students have adopted the black demand for participation in hiring and firing teachers, Marwell feels com-pelled to defend his "liberal" university. "Why do you want to destroy it?. . . . You might turn one of the nation's ten or twelve great research institutions into the University of Wyoming or North Texas State." He departs for his after-noon classes amid Bronx cheers.

Perhaps softened by this send-off, he decides that this is not a good day to conduct business as usual. During his 2:25 class, Marwell allows four black students to lead a heated discussion about the merits of the strike. Afterward he muses, "I guess some students learned. Perhaps more than in most classes. But how many classes can I spend this way?" Never-theless, he turns over the podium of his 3:30 class to a black athlete for another round of discussion. In the late afternoon he wearily stumbles into the "liberated" departmental office, where a handful of unfamiliar students are sprawled across desks and tables. Assured that the liberation is more symbolic than real, Marwell mopes about the university's sudden growth, which has made the anonymity of the sit-in possible. "Today I probably know half of our graduate students and a fiftieth of our undergraduates." Later, at a 5 P.M. academic senate meeting, he finds himself siding with the "student-oriented left wing" of the faculty. "Although I don't like the strike, I don't like the looks on the faces of the faculty either. Not liking the tactics is no reason for turning away from programs which have merit."

Broiling in his ambivalence, he returns home for a brief respite. He catches the "Laugh-In" and a few short hours of sleep before returning to the office at 6 A.M. as monitor of a waning sit-in. He senses that the earlier faculty monitors, enjoying the guitars and underground movies, had struck up an "easy camaraderie [with students] based on shared hardship." Now, at dawn, everyone is too fatigued to talk, so Marwell begins grading a dissertation which arrived on Monday. "The strike has done at least one student some good. Normally I couldn't have gotten to the dissertation for almost two weeks."

Comes the new day, and though the strike goes on, the professorial urge for normality asserts itself. In a final soliloquy, composed at home the evening before, Marwell portrays the university as caught in a pincer-movement between striking students and screaming politicians. "Is this a sinking ship?" he wonders as he thinks about an attractive offer to go elsewhere. "If this is to be no better an intellectual environment than any other, perhaps I should go where the money is? There are students to teach at every university."

The professor's diary, like a fossil on display at a natural history museum, contains the clue to a whole species. The American professor is a modern evolutionary phenomenon. He has become sympathetic yet detached; an admirer of students more in the abstract than the flesh; a loyal member of the department with eyes roving elsewhere. What makes him such a fragile specimen is the fact that his status, and million-miler air wings, are so newly acquired. His beggar's cloak is now replaced by tweeds. His shuffling, gangling manner *à la* Ichabod Crane is now covered over with the élan of a world consultant-statesman-entrepreneur. He hungers for two cars in the garage, two graduate students in the lab, and an endowed chair where he can rest his weary reputation. The nineteenth century professor was placed in charge of both the student's mind and body, a tutor and housemother rolled into one. The modern professor spends as little time as possible with undergraduates. He's a mobile father who, while achieving fame and fortune downtown, bristles at the suggestion that he should be responsible for the kids at home.

The advent of student power has thus caught the faculty in a state of retreat, and its response has been accordingly confused, defensive, and often vicious. Above all else, a professor wants to quietly do his work; the activist wants that work to consist of "doing." The result, building up slowly, is bitter divisiveness. Without a willingness to honestly work with students, and without the machinery to resolve the inevitable crises, the faculty quickly exhausts its limited supply of "liberal" good will and turns recklessly to simple, authoritarian solutions. Schools that have come under the gun develop an ugly, self-perpetuating cycle. A crisis is followed by halfhearted reforms, which are followed by another crisis, which is followed by more punitive reforms.

The classic case of the decaying student-faculty relationship is Berkeley, where the faculty once sympathized with the activists. The famed resolution of December 8, 1964, passed overwhelmingly by the Berkeley academic senate, not only upheld free speech but urged in its very first clause

amnesty for all students "connected with the current controversy over political speech and activity." Thereafter, the
senate established a select committee, which produced the
Muscatine Report, a monumental volume that was to become
a prototype for dozens of committees elsewhere. It declared
grandly: "In the history of American higher education, there
have never been so many ideas and experiments in educational innovation, both outside and within this campus, as
those which clamour at present for study and possible trial."

Following the report's major recommendation, the faculty
senate established the Board of Educational Development
"to stimulate and promote experimentation . . . in all sectors
of the Berkeley campus." Composed of six faculty members,
one chancellor's representative, and no students, the BED
approved over seventy-five experimental courses for credit
during the next three years (1966–1968). It screened and
evaluated new courses so thoroughly that many became
integrated into regular departmental programs. Nevertheless,
BED members worried about getting into political trouble
with some of their more daring field-study projects, which
sent students into the Oakland ghettos or on the Poor People's
March as "participant observers." Since students could not
participate directly on the BED, they formed their own
Center for Participant Education (CPE) in 1967 to submit
proposals to the BED.

In the late summer of 1968, the CPE proposed for the
fall a course on racism built around Eldridge Cleaver, the
author and Black Panther Minister. It was finally approved
by the BED after undergoing the most thorough screening
for academic credibility of any experimental course. It would
have a select enrollment, four faculty sponsors to grade
papers, and a long reading list. Cleaver, who would deliver

ten lectures on "Dehumanization and Regeneration of the Social Order," intended it to be a low-keyed, scholarly affair investigating the effects of oppression on various ethnic and racial groups. When first contacted, the prison-educated Cleaver accepted the invitation to be a guest lecturer enthusiastically. "Once I become a teacher," he grinned, "maybe my mother will think I've come to something." He also felt the opportunity would be beneficial for his parole record.

Publically, Cleaver was an outspoken defender of black self-determination, but he made it clear to his first class that he would be a teacher and not a Black Panther Minister. "I will depart from my regular approach to the microphone," he explained. Although apt to place four-letter words in front of the name Ronald Reagan, he said "I am not here to be a demagogue." Furthermore, Cleaver is one of those rare black men who can relate to whites without forfeiting blackness. At one point, he had to pacify a delegation of Afro-American students who objected to his lecturing a class of honkies.

Despite the precautions taken in setting up the course, and Cleaver's own restrained attitude, Social Analysis 139X became a political issue in early September, three weeks before school began. Trying to announce the course delicately, the public information office, working in conjunction with the BED, put out a disastrous release on September 10 that failed to make clear that Cleaver would only be a guest lecturer, not a staff member. Subsequent clarifying releases were drowned out in a chorus of criticism led by Ronald Reagan. At the monthly meeting on September 20, ten days before school was to open, the regents stepped on a faculty perogative by voting that in a course for credit ". . . no one may lecture or lead a discussion for more than one occasion during a given academic quarter" unless he holds an appointment.

The faculty was quite horrified by this language, mainly because it affected some 200 regular courses that frequently used outside speakers. In the next few weeks, the vice-chancellor handed out 200 lectureships. Cleaver, of course, was not included, although he was eventually allowed to lecture in a not-for-credit course. Naturally the students turned to the faculty, which had established the BED to insist that credit be granted.

However, the faculty did not want to defend the students to the regents. Richard Powell, a flamboyant chemistry professor and chairman of the senate, declared, "I'm a great believer in academic freedom, but I just don't want the faculty to go down on Eldridge Cleaver." For the students, the issues were much more clearly drawn. On October 3, the day when the senate was meeting to deliberate the Cleaver matter, the *Daily Cal* editorialized: "The faculty today will either make a very strong defense for Eldridge Cleaver, the four instructors sponsoring Social Analysis 139X, the Board of Educational Development, the Center for Participant Education, student participation in the educational process, faculty autonomy over courses and curriculum, academic freedom, progress in the University's relations with minority groups and the advancement of equality and freedom in America, or else they will equivocate, procrastinate, masturbate and desecrate the university. There are no other alternatives."

As hundreds stood vigil outside Wheeler Hall, the faculty procrastinated. After four hours of debate they barely managed to break a right-wing filibuster by a compromise measure which committed them only "to take all appropriate steps necessary to assure . . . credit status for the course." "All appropriate steps" meant negotiation. But since the resolution was so toothless, the regents would hardly even discuss the matter. The 40 students finally enrolled in Social Analysis 139X did not receive credit.

Then the faculty proceeded to aid the chancellor's office in the demolition of the Board of Educational Development. Of the twenty respectable courses proposed to the BED for the post-Cleaver winter quarter of 1969, only five were approved. Thereafter the students stopped suggesting courses, and the BED chairman, sickened by the crackdown on innovation, resigned. In the end, the faculty wound up with an atrophied BED and with repressive new regents' by-laws that inhibited their traditional autonomy on course credits and outside speakers.

The pattern at Berkeley, a general model for other campuses, can be reduced to four succeeding stages, like what happens in an internal-combustion engine. In the first stage (at Berkeley in 1964 and at Columbia in 1968), the students lead an impassioned charge against a rigid administration. The faculty, feeling a bit guilty at this point, tries to patch up the schism.

This leads to stage two, a temporary reconstruction, where the faculty sets up a high-powered task force (the Muscatine Committee at Berkeley; the Sovern Executive Faculty Committee at Columbia) to find a mechanism for feeding idealistic student impulses into the system. Inevitably, these committees don't really accomplish anything. Their shiny reports make good reading in the mass media, but they are not really taken to heart at home. Or rather, they are taken to heart by too many footnote-trained scholars who niggle over recommendations while their schools prepare to blow up again. Columbia probably set a new world's record by taking one year and fifteen drafts to establish a new unicameral senate with limited authority where students will be outnumbered four to one.

In stage three, the students, tired of faculty procrastination, turn on their mentors by using a strategy of selective class disruption to win support for demands. The faculty responds with varying degrees of bitterness. At Berkeley and Wisconsin early in 1969, the academic senates supported the administration's handling of the disturbances, including the excessive use of police and national guardsmen.

Stage three is critical because it marks the shift in faculty sentiment from a feeling that amnesty and reform are the answer to a belief that only sharp discipline will work. In this atmosphere, the reforms of stage two are replaced by punishment. The scrapping of the BED at Berkeley this past year was one example. At Wisconsin, the Crow Committee on student participation in university governance was established in August of 1967 during phase two, after the early, mild anti-Dow demonstrations of the previous February. By the time the report was completed and implemented in October, 1968, a second and more "obstructive" sit-in had occurred, so the report became the basis for new disciplinary tribunals. Columbia's new senate can likewise be expected to shatter after sustained stage-three disruptions. In fact, there was evidence during the spring, even before the senate was established, that faculty patience was beginning to wear thin. After several classes were disrupted in late February of 1969, a special group of senior professors issued a strong statement denouncing the disruption and urging campus tribunals to "demonstrate the will to act." In the eventuality of another major uprising at Columbia, the professors (the majority of the senate) will probably want to use it as a forum for castigating the rebels; the moderate, elected students will be so appalled at the faculty's vindictiveness that they will undoubtedly walk out en masse. The faculty will now have total control of what it wanted in the first place: a strong, independent organ for asserting its own rights.

The fourth stage is one of tranquility and reconstruction —briefly. The faculty makes some kind of response to student demands (by setting up a black studies department at Wisconsin, an ethnic college at Berkeley), but it will not part with its fundamental power-monopoly, which underlies the whole academic imbalance. The stage four reconstruction brings the faculty full circle back to stage one in the sense that it is still willing to support students on off-campus non-academic issues. At the end of the 1968–69 school year, the faculties of both Berkeley and Wisconsin were as a whole sympathetic to students as they battled police for control of "The People's Park" at Berkeley and the right to hold a "Mifflin Street" block party at Wisconsin. However, this temporary support will no doubt dissolve as students begin to press academic issues once again in the fall. Thereafter, the second and fourth reconstruction stages will probably become far more spasmodic while the third punishment stage becomes much more sustained.

The final irony is that the faculty has profited from its experiences with student power. As student politics expert Seymour M. Lipset of Harvard says, "From what I know of Berkeley, I'd say the biggest structural change that's occurred there since the Free Speech Movement of 1964, particularly among the social sciences, is that the faculty is teaching much less." Thus relieved of the teaching burden, the professor feels secure. Lipset adds, "You can't expect to change the system in any given school, because if you succeed in getting any one university to put pressure on its scholars to emphasize teaching, they'll just quit—there are plenty of other universities which will give higher salaries and lighter teaching loads to recruit prestigious scholars."

Lipset himself is an example of his own thesis that a faculty man would rather switch than fight. Or rather, that he can switch and then continue to wage the fight even better from afar. Like Lipset, a whole bevy of student specialists have left Berkeley for more placid climes, where they continue to rant about the horrors of campus conflict. Lewis Feuer, the sociologist, now at Toronto, has probably made the biggest splash with his Freudian analyses of student unrest. Even William Bouwsma, the historian and vice-chancellor, who labored so diligently to repulse Ivy League recruiters, has at long last succumbed himself and is taking up residence at Harvard in the fall of 1969. It is always amusing to hear commentators decry the mobility of protestors. The professor who can't take the heat need only pack up his family and move elsewhere. The student who is summarily kicked out of school has no such opportunity.

But even on calmer campuses, an internal threat remains. For all his pretensions about being independent and open-minded, the professor is fearful. Like the blue-collar worker who has moved up to the suburbs, he still doesn't feel quite comfortable in his new setting. For there are imposters who feel that without earning the privilege they can move in next door and depreciate the departmental property value. These are the assistant professors, young men who enjoy teaching, maintain good rapport with students, talk loudly at department meetings, and ostentatiously join the latest sit-in. Their scholarship is lost in simple moralism. They lack "detachment." In short, they're a threat that must be put down.

There is one dilemma. The senior faculty man does not

like scenes. Like all his colleagues, he is a professional, a reasonable man. He adheres to professorial etiquette and is a member of the AAUP* country club. So when a radical professor comes up for tenure or reappointment, no one gets up in public and says, "I can't stand this presumptuous fucker." Instead, the senior men of the department gather privately and decide whether a man is "professional" enough to be retained. Professionalism is to scholars what efficiency is to administrators, the catch-all, end-all, be-all of their purposes. Thus, when an assistant English professor at a small Midwestern college used material from *Evergreen Review* in his freshman composition course, he was not rehired, because he had "failed to develop the professional discipline that molds an inexperienced instructor into an effective teacher." At Michigan a virulent antiwar chemist connected with a solid research program was denied tenure after four and a half years. The reasons remained "privileged information," unknown even to him. The victim has no right to appeal.

In an effort to protect these and other "anonymous victims of the New McCarthyism," an organization called the New University Conference has been established with headquarters near the University of Chicago campus. (One of its charter members, Mrs. Marlene Dixon, was herself involved in a celebrated case in 1969.) In a statement of purpose, the NUC outlined the dilemma of radical scholars: "They have been told that they have not published enough by departments which have promoted those who publish less. They have been told that their scholarship was merely derivative by men who are praised for writing 'brilliant syntheses.' They have been told that they have not worked for an academic

*American Association of University Professors.

audience by those whose work is classified. . . . They have been told that their convictions interfere with their scholarship in departments where full professors boasted that their scholarship is their way of fighting communism."

The radical professor does not break with the system overnight. Marlene Dixon, the deposed sociology professor at the University of Chicago, worked within the academic system all the way through graduate school. Her activism, up to that point, had been directed toward civil rights issues off campus. As a doctoral candidate at UCLA, she was engrossed in an investigation of the engineering profession, a project of great interest to her department chairman and thesis director. As her specialty was survey research, she arrived at Chicago with mounds of data. Within six months, she "realized that I was bored with survey research . . . and it was [only] to some sense of obligation for what you do with collected materials that I kept poking at them." She felt she was becoming academically schizophrenic, trying "not to be one thing in public and another thing in one's work."

Even as she began exploring the shortcomings of pluralism, the bases of imperialism and class structure, there was still ingrained in her, by training, the importance of not misusing the podium or taking advantage of a captive audience. "I would describe what my biases were, and if I felt very polemical about something, and decided I wanted to be polemical, I would step away from the podium and I would tell the students 'I have stepped away from the podium. I am now going to be polemical. You should note that . . . I'm stepping out of the magic circle.' And then I would thunder to my heart's content." The Gray Committee, the special faculty panel that investigated her nonrenewal, was told by almost all students they consulted "that she made clear her radical biases but dissociated them from her systematic presentation. Some students who explicitly disagreed with her views stressed that they felt under no constraint, and indeed were encouraged to voice their own views." In summary, the committee report stated, "Our general conclusion is that Mrs. Dixon is an energetic, warm, dedicated, open and compelling teacher."

To the Chicago sociology department, only a very special kind of scholarship is "professional." Mrs. Dixon's teaching and future scholarship potential were not enough.* When she foolishly gave permission for a public appraisal of her work, the department used their most distinguished member, Edward Shils, commuting from Cambridge, England, to give her a special evalution. "Mrs. Dixon's level of performance," he concluded from her incomplete portfolio, is at best unqualifiedly mediocre. She has not a single relatively original or even bold idea. She has not pursued a central theme with rigor nor depth." Once the case had blown up in headlines all over America, no other top-quality American sociology department would hire her. She will wind up at McGill University in Canada.

What really brings such anathema on radical teachers? Is it the usual stated reasons—their scholarship, their histrionic teaching? Or is it more personal factors, the disappointment of a father whose son doesn't want to join the family business or wants the old family business to diversify?

The case of Larry Caroline at the University of Texas is a chilling example. The twenty-eight-year-old Caroline, built like a basketball center, was a philosopher specializing in ethics and political philosophy. He came to Texas as an assistant professor with high marks from his home institution, the

*Mrs. Dixon is a leader of the Women's Liberation movement. Women activists protested that she was put down more for her sex than her radicalism.

University of Michigan. Like Mrs. Dixon, Caroline was not a typical academic product. He, too, sought to link radicalism and professionalism. He became faculty sponsor of SDS and exerted a strong moderating force against the Peking-oriented Progressive Labor Party. Like Mrs. Dixon, he enjoyed teaching. For example, during one quarter he divided up his introductory ethics course of 150 students into ten sections and, at his chairman's insistence, personally led every section. In class he did not play the professorial superiority game, but preferred to interact Socratically, severely challenging the basic premise of philosophy's search for the Great Reality. "You'll find SDS meetings more fun than this class," he kidded a visitor. While he obviously became popular with radicals, many conservative students also enjoyed sparring with him. One very prim and proper freshman from Dallas paid Caroline a Texas-style compliment. "Take away the beard and he's just like William Buckley. If he gets you in his jaws, he'll tear you apart." Unfortunately, Caroline was still ABD (all but dissertation) and, without a doctorate, ineligible to teach graduate seminars. Some senior professors attributed his popularity with frosh to the fact that he was "all charisma and no content."

"Perhaps the most controversial aspect of Larry Caroline was his attempt to mix politics and philosophy. His most explosive mixture was at an antiwar rally on the steps of the state capitol in Austin in October, 1967. There he said that this country needs a revolution—but not necessarily a "bloody" one. Some people in the crowd were horrified by his bluntness; most were ecstatic. One girl rushed up and kissed him. The speech, spectacularized and misquoted, made headlines. Frank Erwin, the powerful Democratic chairman of the regents, told the *Houston Post* five days later, "I'm absolutely outraged that any teaching employee would do such a thing and I'm going to do something about it." The administration quietly explored ways to cut his name off the budget line. Then, unwilling to create an academic-freedom hassle, it backed off under legal advice.

The most disturbed man was the philosophy department chairman, John R. Silber, who was to take over as Dean of Arts and Sciences on November 1, 1968. Gutsy and irascible, capable of lacing the most delicate philosophic argument with the most flatulent expletive, John Silber is an ex-radical for whom the God has failed. As a young philosophy professor in the fifties he had been censured and almost fired by the regents for advocating integration. During the formative years of SDS on campus, he had served as faculty advisor. As department chairman, he had been a vigorous recruiter of good young teachers. Hence his enthusiasm for Caroline.

But like many veteran activists, Silber had not been able to negotiate the transition to civil disobedience. "The radicals," he raged on day in his office, "take the position that they can walk all over you and all over due process procedures with a Marcusean logic that the truth and higher good will emerge later. That's just well-poisoning. We fought to extend the law equally to all parties. SDS today has become an enemy of the law." To Silber, Caroline was part of this despicable trend. "To convince Larry Caroline that he has free speech, I have to congratulate him on every ridiculous statement he makes. Well, I have a very low tolerance for bullshit." Above all, Silber believed that a philosopher cannot operate on "blind moral zeal."

If Caroline had retreated from public forums and completed his pending thesis, the entire episode might have blown over. However, Caroline was not the type of person to bow to silly conventions. Since no one asked about the thesis, he assumed that "the timetable was to get the thing finished on the day it's done." He threw himself into his teaching, and would not abandon his antiwar preaching. "I can't play by their rules," he vowed. "They'd corrupt me overnight."

The Caroline case welled up and spilled over in the spring. At the beginning of the term, Caroline had prevailed upon Silber, as Dean, to admit a Negro youth named Larry Jackson, a SNCC organizer, who was at the bottom of his high school class and a low achiever on his college boards. Silber cajoled the registrar into admitting Jackson, but only after an agreement with Caroline that he would tutor the youth. However, Jackson disliked school; Caroline refused to press him; Silber felt his pact with Caroline had been broken. When Jackson dropped out of school in early April (under pressure from Silber to drop out rather than flunk out), the Silber-Caroline relationship was beginning to crumble. At that same time, Martin Luther King was assassinated.

On Friday, April 5, 1968, a memorial service for Martin Luther King was followed by a march of mourners and protesters from the university to the state capitol. One speaker, an ardent SDS member, accused the university—and Silber, among others—of racism. This was becoming a catchall pejorative, denial of which only created further embarrassment. Silber tried to defend himself, citing his own integrationist record and pointing out that he was in the process of hiring a Negro secretary. The crowd became indignant. Following Silber to the microphone, Larry Caroline said, "The time for white people to define the truth for black people is past," a statement that applied to himself as much as anyone else. Silver never forgave Caroline for that day in the capitol rotunda or for the whole Larry Jackson affair.

In May, at a stormy four-hour meeting of the philosophy department budget council, Silber gave his account of the Jackson affair and the rotunda speech. "The failure of a philosopher to say anything in order to put the record straight in a moment like that is a pretty serious betrayal of his responsibilities.... I think that this kind of sell-out, an accommodation in order to maintain one's political position and his public image, is unworthy of anybody that takes truth seriously." While Silber granted Caroline's "competence in the classroom" and "other aspects of Larry Caroline which are extraordinarily attractive," this was barely discussed. The issue hinged on the so-called discrepancies between the private philosophical man and the public radical. Another strong opponent of Caroline asked, "What have I got here? Have I got a guy who is a whole man, or who inhabits a classroom of Waggener Hall M W F at 10:00, and then becomes a political tactician?"

The more radical members of the department, or those who tried to understand Caroline in a radical context, were not disturbed by these discrepancies. One professor, who had spent several hours on that very day discussing political philosophy with Caroline, concluded, "I didn't find any remarkable use of fallacious argumentation or anything of the sort —certainly not more than in any of the rest of us."

After not renewing his contract, the department decided to postpone final action on renewal until fall, 1968. This time Silber stayed out of the department decision. A new department chairman, Irwin Lieb, courted votes against Caroline. Graduate students were warmed with a beer bust, junior faculty were invited to the budget council, senior men got special briefings on the matter. But the politicking failed, and the senior faculty voted six to five for a two-year extension of Caroline's contract. Having lost democratically, the new chairman proceeded to recommend to Silber (now Dean of the college) that Caroline's contract not be renewed because of "obvious conflict in the department." Dean Silber upheld this decision, and President Norman Hackerman concurred. Larry Caroline was out.

Of course, not all younger professors are trouble-makers. Kenneth Dolbeare, a moderate radical and up-and-coming political scientist at Wisconsin, noted that he was a valuable source of intelligence for the somewhat stodgy dean. "Even my colleagues have gotten used to the idea of having all the beards on campus lined up outside my office. They'll make comments like—'Hey, we liked those dogs that were roaming around the corridors.'" Like Dolbeare, who is an associate professor, many a younger teacher wins brownie points by performing boring household tasks, such as revising the undergraduate curriculum. Here too, he can score points on both sides of the net—from students for liberalizing the requirements, and from colleagues for quietly lobbying the revisions through the departmental councils.

The department is a versatile organism. It is a curator of the latest research technology. It is also a very primitive social system offering an impregnable territorial defense against outsiders, whether they be politicians, administrators, or undergraduates; internally, the department functions as effectively as a Mafia family. The young are kept under control by tight reward-and-sanction mechanisms, such as grades for undergraduates, doctoral puberty rites for graduate students, and tenure for assistant professors. Likewise, the elders of the tribe have built up a series of conventions that foster nonaggressive behavior, despite the fact that Marxists and capitalists may share the same cubicle. For example, personal property such as courses and research, is given sacred sanction; picking on a professor's prized survey course is akin to violating his wife. In making important decisions, departmental councils (normally comprised of elders only) operate on a principle of consensus, whereby the minority never argues so harshly that it can't recant and defer to the majority. In personnel matters, a good department works like a jury to reach unanimity.

At state universities, where working conditions and salaries may not be ideal, unity and reputation are powerful substitutes. Students, if they are permitted access to decision-making levels, can make "trouble" and shatter this precious unity. The struggle within the University of Wisconsin history department this past year should be viewed in that light.

The conflict opened at the first weekly departmental meeting, on September 19, 1968. The department met for lunch in the Old Madison Room, a private dining room decorated with frontier scenes from Old Madison, on the fourth floor of the student union. The men sat in a tightly-knit group around a U-shaped table devouring their tossed salads, chicken pot pies, and fluffy chocolate puddings with whipped cream. Then, while coffee was being served, the chairman called the meeting to order.

Before he could introduce the new faculty members, some unexpected guests arrived. Approximately forty students, many of them carrying green book bags and wearing that lean and hungry look that smacks of radicalism, filed into the room behind their guru, a Marxist professor. Suddenly the room was tense. Several men felt a distinct chicken-pot-pie aftertaste bubbling up in their throats. The chairman nervously announced, "As you can see, there are some students here." One faculty member who had loosened his belt to make room for the whipped cream decided to buckle up and look dignified. The Marxist professor, embarrassed by dirty looks from colleagues, walked over and sat behind the food service table.

Finally the new men were introduced, and endless announcements were made about upcoming conferences ("The Impact of the Fifth Republic on France" conference would be held in mid-Otober). Then the department settled down to the main item on the agenda, a discussion of motions to set up student-faculty committees that could advise the department on curriculums and teaching improvements.

Several students sought permission to speak on the motions. One historian, an Englishman, denounced them as "intruders." The chairman noted that permission for non-faculty members to participate required unanimous consent. The parliamentarian upheld this ruling. A forty-five minute discussion ensued on whether the students should be allowed to speak. They were finally granted an hour, by voice vote. The Englishman and several others abstained so as to permit unanimity.

William Kaplan, a senior, identified himself as a member of the History Students Association, a "revolutionary group" whose purpose "is to destroy capitalism." He denounced the proposed advisory committees as tokens. Citing the blood-curdling example of Columbia, he said that "there might not be a university here to operate" if the faculty failed to create committees with "decision-making power." A more moderate student denounced Kaplan and the HSA as "commies." A plump economic historian warned that though student participation is desirable, he "does not think any [faculty] members are dedicated to the use of the department for the transformation of society by revolutionary action this year."

At 3:10 P.M. the faculty unanimously voted, "in the spirit of a community of scholars," that two student-faculty committees would be created, one for undergraduates and one for graduates. The meeting adjourned. The students reluctantly left, and the tenured men stayed for a brief executive committee session. Shortly after 4 P.M., the senior men returned to their scholarly activities. This is the way the department repulses what it believes to be a heathen invasion.

The Wisconsin history department, one of the nation's best, is especially susceptible because it is large, overcrowded, and heavily endowed with graduate-student instructors, so that many professors go several years at a time without ever conducting an exclusively undergraduate class. At the same time, its excellent reputation draws bright, urban students—the stuff from which radicals are molded.

History majors had been prominent in the 1967 Dow demonstration, which had come to a bloody conclusion when the cops brutally cleared Bascom Hall. Perhaps because they were so aware of the futility of having their heads busted again, some activists seized upon the tactic of "departmental organizing" in the fall of 1968, forming the History Student Association which would work within the system until such time as links with outside forces could be formed. While many of the hard-line radicals sneered at this "reformist tactic," the general sentiment in the fall was certainly against violence. During the week of the national presidential election in November, the massive antiwar forces on campus settled for a mild symbolic protest.

Like any fledgling organization, the HSA opened its fall offensive with a pamphlet manifesto, offering a critique and program that blended wit and wisdom. The cover carried a cartoon showing a bespectacled HSA member peeking under the skirt of Clio, the buxom muse of history. The introductory page declared solemnly: "Students of the world UNITE! You have nothing to lose but your grades." The pamphlet noted that as a discipline, history is far too self-congratulatory—at the expense of analysis. The emphasis on elite leaders as movers of history, the framework of gradual change, tended to "channel students into the government bureaucracy and existing political parties by emphasizing either the futility or destructiveness of conflict and revolutionary movements."

The major thrust of the pamphlet was aimed at the department as an authoritarian system. From a radical perspective, it saw the department structure as the work of men who wanted to fragment and compartmentalize undergraduates as neatly as they chop up pre- and post-1865 history. Graduate students fortunate enough to become teaching assistants suffered further degradations. The report cited one math professor who supplied her TAs with a list of "do's and don'ts" which included: "Don't address students by their first names." "Don't chew gum while teaching." "Don't be influenced by attractive students of the opposite sex when giving grades."

HSA pamphleteering was not very well received. One professor denounced the HSA literature as "pornography." Another moped, "Here I've spent three days trying to find jobs for my graduate students and all I read about is how I sit in a Frank Lloyd Wright home with a large stereo console." David Cronon, known as "Chairman Cronon" in the manifesto, was particularly upset. In his office, under a portrait of the department's second chairman, Frederick Jackson Turner, he offered his own critique of the university. "This is a very unbureaucratic kind of place," he explained. "From a faculty viewpoint you can pretty much do what you want."

He scoffed at the notion that he was part of a small ruling clique. "I'm just a traffic cop making sure we don't have too many courses in the same intersection."

When the students began regularly attending departmental meetings, citing a state antisecrecy statute, Cronon became distraught as much out of awkwardness as of fear. At the podium he would scratch his crew cut, redden, and strike a sardonic pose that only made him look more supercilious to the students. He had hoped that the student-faculty committees, established at the first meeting, would be sufficient concessions to student demands for participation. Then he discovered that the HSA intended to make a regular habit of attending departmental meetings. "The radicals won't be assuaged by any means," he angrily fretted. "If you give them one piece of the pie, they want the whole pie. If you give them the whole pie, they want another pie." Trying to quash their interest in the meetings, he used a very powerful weapon— boredom. "Normally at our early meetings there isn't much business," he chuckled. "But because I didn't want the students to think we were hiding anything, I dredged up everything, all the fellowship announcements I could find and had the longest, dullest agenda probably since the department was organized."

Of course the HSA was barred from important departmental discussions. In October, when an assistant professor allowed his class to set up an A or F grading system (similar to pass-fail), the department met in closed executive session on the absurd grounds that this was a personnel matter because it "concerned a person." (Normally personnel matters deal with promotions, appointments and salaries.) Before the meeting, some 400 students staged a brief sit-in, which was cut short by the chairman's threat to initiate disciplinary proceedings against the protestors if they disrupted the meeting. The students backed off, and the executive committee issued only a slight reprimand to the young professor by forbidding future grade experimentation without permission.

The tension pervading the history department was duplicated across campus. A dozen similar radical student associations were working in sociology, anthropology, even engineering. It was inevitable that a spark would ignite this smoldering unrest. In February the radical students fell in behind black leadership for a chaotic, weeklong strike highlighted by a special deployment of 2,000 Wisconsin National Guardsmen. While the demands were black-oriented, there is little doubt that the momentum of the strike was sustained by hundreds of white militants in the various departmental associations. In the history department, the student association pressured the faculty into a pledge of "full cooperation in the setting up of a black studies department." In sociology, when the department did not act quickly enough, a group of some sixty students (which dwindled to fifteen) staged an all-night sit-in in the departmental office. In economics, anthropology, philosophy, and journalism, the students summoned their professors to take a stand on the strike and made demands that included the right of black students to have veto power over the hiring and firing of teachers and administrators in the new department.

Significantly, the white students recognized that in striking for the black demands they were setting a precedent for their own visions of student power. "What we can't get for ourselves," explained an economics student, "we'll get for them. Then, we'll get it for ourselves." Recognizing this threat, the departments responded with tepid resolutions supporting less controversial demands, such as the recruiting of more black students.

This is not to suggest that the departmental organizers, a small group among thousands of strikers, were the only dynamos of the strike. Rather, they gave it a distinct style. Working with the black leadership, they helped fashion a new bull's-eye—the faculty—on the perennial target of racism. Although the administration was burned in effigy and bitterly condemned for calling the troops, the tactics of the strike were mainly directed at the faculty. Instead of the isolated Columbia-type tactics, in which one or two buildings are seized, the strikers swept through several classroom buildings. Instead of simply confronting the cops by mass obstruction, they asked their professors (who claim to uphold free speech) to take time out from zoology lectures to permit discussion of strike issues. And instead of simply seeking overall faculty support in the academic senate (*à la* Berkeley, 1964), they went to the real grass roots—the departments—forced the faculty to vote through a black studies department that included student participation. Until the strike, the topic had been log-jammed in faculty committees for nine months.

In the history department, some progress was made. At a special meeting called during the strike, the department appeared willing to act on the controversies surrounding the university. It supported the admission of "academically-qualified" blacks who had been expelled from Oshkosh State in a November protest. It pledged "full cooperation in the setting up of a Black Studies Department."

Conceivably, this meeting might have been the crucible from which a new bond of cooperation would be forged. However, many of the more conservative professors were quietly smouldering at the endorsement of "non-departmental issues" raised by the strike. In addition, some students had used blunt language in condemning faculty members. One HSA leader, a bit carried away, cried out, "You're full of bullshit. B-U-L-L-S-H-I-T." For those men looking for an excuse to crack down, this was it.

Quietly, in small home caucuses, the conservatives began organizing. "Now it's our turn to put these motherfuckers up against the war," they would almost gleefully tell colleagues in the corridors. On March 6 some twenty-eight names were on a motion that barred students (excepting certified representatives) from all future departmental meetings. It passed twenty-four to sixteen. Professor Ted Hamerow, who introduced it, later told the HSA that he did so because he objected to "intimidation, violence, insult and obscenity at faculty meetings. We are told if we don't do something, we are missing certain parts of our anatomy." The next day, the moderates tried to retrench by pushing the chairman to appoint a new faculty committee to explore ways of bettering student relations. Cronon agreed—appointing himself, naturally, as chairman of a new seven-man panel. It eventually decided to set up a new student assembly for the department (as well as special student committees on fellowships and curriculum, etc.), but there was no provision for students to attend faculty meetings.

The HSA, closed out from meetings by the March sixth motion, threatened to bring suit under the state's anti-secrecy statute....

The HSA retaliated by denouncing the faculty's "ahistorical view of social change" and announcing that it would bring suit, under the state's antisecrecy statute, to reopen the meetings. Briefly, for one passionate evening, there was even talk of further sit-ins. But, as one student confessed, "A certain paralysis has set in. We don't have the time to play these games and get ready for finals." Any further direct action was deferred. The year had taken its toll on the consensus-minded department as well, which now had a feeling of being both virgin and violated at the same time. Several members entertained offers and hopes of going to "a more humane setting where we can teach undergraduates." Many others, including the chairman, were conveniently scheduled to go on leave the next semester. Some older men still mouthed the same certitudes in June that they had used in September. "This department cannot be in the business of sponsoring revolution," said one. "We're here to study history."

# CHAPTER 3:

# THE ADMINISTRATION

The sheaves of memorandums, representing tomorrow's problems, piled up on the desk of Cornell President James Perkins as he struggled to wade through the present day's crowded morning calendar. The docket was filled with students. First the white radicals had an appointment to discuss their proposal of a student-run course for credit. Perkins listened to the idea, probed its merits, and then swiftly disposed of it with a nifty bureaucratic shuffle. "You've come to the right church but the wrong pew," he declared, draping his jowls into a poker face to underscore his one-liner. With a wave of his hand Perkins pointed to the proper cleric, the academic vice-president, who had come to the president's office expecting to talk about the reorganization of the political science department. And with that the first crisis of the day was over.

Next on the agenda was a black leader, so Perkins walked out into the foyer to meet him. Spotting only a white administrative aide, he chortled, "You certainly don't look like Paul DuBois." In midsentence he realized that the young black was standing within earshot, partially hidden, talking to a typist. "Oh, Paul," Perkins recovered smoothly, "there you are, making it with the secretaries again." Paul, in a three-piece suit, silently followed the white-haired president back to his office.

When his foyer was finally bare, Perkins was free to devote a few minutes to paper work. He contemplated a snappy reply to an Arkansas alumnus who had complained about beatniks in the bleachers of the Colgate-Cornell game. He concluded arrangements with the Ford Foundation that would let him take a student along to a major educational conference in Germany. He gave a quick glance at an SDS document called "Who Rules Cornell" and underlined the inaccuracies.

It was nearly noon; there was barely time to walk over to a luncheon meeting in the Red Barn, a converted coach house that had belonged to Andrew White, the first Cornell president. Perkins was hosting there a select group of clean-cut seniors picked by the alumni association as part of a quarterly program called "Cornell in Perspective." After a meal of tuna salad and tomatoes, Perkins stood up and flashed his poker look. "As President," he said, "I do not have the answers to some of your questions—only an enormous capacity to dispose of them." The group smiled appreciatively. After a grueling morning, Perkins had found his element. That was

Jim Perkins in November, 1968: a smile, a wink, and a rollicking platitude.

In December the Afro-American Society took a militant turn and began a series of small-scale agitations; by January they had mushroomed into a major campus judiciary crisis. Tensions escalated during the spring. The blacks occupied Willard Straight Hall in April and eventually imported guns for self-protection. When they emerged, protected by an amnesty agreement signed by the administration, guns raised in triumph, the campus and nation recoiled in horror. *The New York Times* reported that Perkins' law-and-order faculty were in revolt. The DA began a grand jury probe. The normally benign trustees started their own investigation of Perkins' leniency.

Now red-eyed, tired, and distracted, Perkins carried on like Lyndon Johnson preparing for his final days. In the middle of one serious conversation, Perkins stood up, went to the window, looked over a construction site and sighed. "You know, the only thing that has made it all worthwhile is the bookstore going up over there."

Like his old Swarthmore friend and soccer teammate Clark Kerr, Perkins was the ideal multiversity president. He served as the "mediator-initiator" seeking the "workable compromise" between competitive campus factions in order to reconcile the "values of the past, the prospects for the future and the realities of the present." The Kerr-type president, defined in his famous Godkin Lectures at Harvard in 1963, was not merely a "two-faced character," but rather a "many-faced character," hopping around like a karate brown belt, "contriving to turn his back on no important group." The Perkins-type president was defined in his imitative series of Stafford Little Lectures at Princeton in 1965. At that time

he declared: "University integrity is involved not with pre-
serving things as they are, but rather with maintaining the
coherence of its various parts, and the harmony with which
it is able to pursue its aims—whatever their specialized nature." Like a pastor, Perkins would guide his flock toward
progress with togetherness.

The first commandmant of enlightened mediation was,
"keep talking"—in the hope that communication would
deter combustion. Personal diplomacy conducted in a stern
yet wry manner had long been a Perkins trademark. He spent
"unbelievable hours of talking and persuading" and appointed numerous presidential study commissions. As he
explained to a Boston alumni group, the president must try
to anticipate and alleviate "difficulties" so that at least "the
rational center feels you are rational."

In public, Perkins tried to show his rationality by dissecting
the student movement with clinical detachment. On the ban-
quet circuit or educational television, he displayed his "understanding" of activists with historical parallels. "Student
demonstrations began the first day Harvard opened its doors
and the second day at Cornell," he reassured concerned
alumni. For reporters he boiled down the essence of dealing
with activists to quotable formulas. The "quick litmus test
for every admiinstrator," he said sagely, "is whether he knows
the name of the Afro-American Society president. The personal relationship is crucial here because any leader responds
to the knowledge that you recognize him as an individual, not
as a symbol." Perkins was not merely a talker. He personally
launched the Negro opportunity program in 1963, pleaded
to the faculty for student amnesty after a black sit-in in 1968,
and pushed ahead as rapidly as any president in higher education towards the establishment of a black studies center in

the 1968–69 academic year.

And yet quite often the Perkins style seemed geared more to high visibility than to substance, as if his own display of moral courage could compensate for the deficiencies of the structure. When the educational-reform boom struck Cornell in Berkeley's wake, he appointed a "president's commission" on undergraduate education, which turned out yearly progress reports. (Yet a crucial freshman humanities seminar, utilizing many disciplines, has faltered because some departments wouldn't make sufficient manpower available.) When General Hershey announced that draft protestors would face reclassification, Perkins made a special trip to Washington to voice his disapproval. Meanwhile, back on campus, the assistant registrar was caught sending out a special notice to draft boards identifying dissenters.

His usual strategies finally backfired on the issue of South African investments. For more than a year white radicals, and some blacks as well, had complained about Cornell's stock holdings in banks giving loans to "racist" South Africa. Periodically, Perkins would give the standard defense of those investments on the grounds that financial policies were based on monetary and not social factors. To avoid violence, he even brought students and trustees together for a special dinner meeting. But, of course, while he would gladly "explain" the investment policy, he would not consider the possibility of changing it.

At a South Africa symposium in March, he was once again defending the investments when an angry black sophomore standing near the podium grabbed him and pulled him back. His collar (and ego) mussed, Perkins quickly left the stage without further comment. One week later he learned that the bank stocks, in liquidation for more than a year, had all finally been sold more than a month before the symposium. Perkins tried to write off the whole caper by expressing his deep embarrassment, and by pointing out that the treasurer had been on his honeymoon during the week of the symposium. His ignorance suggested that during his ardent year-long defense of the bank investments, he had never pursued the subject with the trustees, nor read the trustee investment reports that he so vigorously defended. Meanwhile, the treasurer, back from his honeymoon, went out of his way to stress that the decision to sell had been based solely on a bearish prognosis for bank stocks. He told the *Cornell Daily Sun,* "If we feel that the bank stocks are cheaper, then we might very well buy them again."

Perkins was still reeling from the "collar incident" when the blacks took over Willard Straight Hall on April 19. That was the Saturday morning of parents weekend. Subordinates found the president "dazed." Unlike Harvard's Nathan Pusey, who acted first and talked later, Perkins went to the opposite extreme and let the situation trickle out of his grasp. He summoned a small group of faculty and students and tried to "implicate" them in a decision, but they didn't want to make one, and he wouldn't act unilaterally. "It was a paralyzing situation," recalled a top administrator. "No one could make up his mind. We weren't going to send the cops, we weren't going to get an injunction and no one was in a hurry to negotiate."

Meanwhile, a fraternity vigilante squad invaded the black sanctuary of the "Straight," and there were endless rumors of armed carloads of other whites on the way. When the blacks imported a dozen weapons for self-protection at dusk Saturday, the situation had reached the breaking point. Early Sunday, two top administrators began negotiations. "It was a matter of life and death," Vice-President Steven Muller recalled later. "When we walked in the black students were both scared and defiant—the classic symptoms of paranoia." The administration ended the occupation with an amnesty agreement. But the campus, still swirling with rumors, saw only the pictures of armed students on the front pages of newspapers on Monday morning.

In an address to the campus that Monday afternoon, Perkins refused to discuss the issues. Instead he spun out a hackneyed plea on the "humane university" that he had been preparing as a Phi Beta Kappa address to be delivered at UCLA. The faculty, more confused than angry, refused to ratify the amnesty agreement when it met later that afternoon. But despite many newspaper accounts of the faculty's "rejection" of the agreement, Perkins was able to salvage a compromise which he had personally drafted. "I was trying to act as *amicus curiae,*" he explained. "So I jotted down what I thought were the points of agreement on an envelope. That formed the basis of the compromise although I had one hell of a time trying to read my writing when it came time to repeat the motion."

It was his final act of conciliation. Thereafter, faculty members and student leaders who had chafed under his buttery style began rejecting his "good offices" and formed a restructuring convocation. Slightly hurt, but keeping a stiff upper lip, Perkins told a faculty leader, "When you restructure this place, I want you to promise me you will eliminate the president's office." A few weeks later, shortly before the end of the term, he resigned.

Perkins at least went down trying. But some presidents, having no turn signals and no reverse gear, continue to drive the same straight line no matter how the times change. As a classicist with a temperament more suitable for a headmaster than a college president, Harvard's Nathan Pusey has long played the role of Moral Philosopher to the college community. Pusey's "deep conviction" of the "essential rightness of Harvard's present orientation" prompted him to ridicule a radical professor in 1961 for living in a "never-never land." A radical of sorts himself in the fifties, when he opposed McCarthyism, Pusey has been unable to adjust to the turbulent radicals of the sixties. In perhaps his most famous excursion into fantasy land he made the following analysis of radicals in his president's report of 1966-67:

". . . they say our universities are now devoted to 'the present and future oppression and domination of the people of the world—both in Vietnam and in our urban ghettoes.' Obviously they live in a world of fantasy . . . within the sanctuary of an ordered society, dreaming of glory—Walter Mittys of the left (or are they left?)—they play at being revolutionaries and fancy themselves rising to positions of command atop the debris as the structures of society come crashing down."

His report went on to explain that in contrast to "the small group bent on destruction . . . the vast majority of Harvard undergraduates went about their essential bsuiness seriously and gaily, as students have done from the beginning. . . ."

Pusey's intellectual orientation makes it easy to understand why the Harvard situation resembles a case of Grayson Kirk's Columbia revisited. Like Kirk, Pusey (despite the fact that his office is sheltered in a freshman dormitory) kept himself closeted from students, particularly radical ones. "I don't have time for radical students," he explained. "I'm too busy working on faculty appointments. I would gladly meet more with students—but how do you choose which ones?" Instead,

Pusey always concentrated on more formal gatherings: his sherry party for seniors; his bi-annual visits to the residential houses; his annual baccalaureate address in the chapel, where he would usually discuss a student theme. (His 1967 topic was "I, Too, Dissent.")

Between baccalaureate addresses, however, he was being eaten alive by Walter Mittys. For example, during the 1968–69 academic year, opposition to ROTC's relationship with Harvard developed in many student and faculty quarters. In February the faculty voted to withdraw academic credit from ROTC. It was a step short of the SDS demand to expel ROTC altogether, but it revealed what the dean called "a desire to go on record against all things military." Pusey publicly chose to interpret the faculty vote as an endorsement of ROTC but privately followed the suggestion of his dean that the vote be skirted by appointing a committee to negotiate with Washington officials. In late March, Pusey made a rare personal appearance when he met with a student-faculty committee discussing the ROTC issue. As usual, the president had his eyes fixed firmly forward. "The current notion that the military-industrial complex is an evil thing does not correspond with reality," he said. After his performance, sociologist Barrington Moore noted with disgust, "This may sound arrogant but I would have to teach him the political alphabet before he could begin to understand the 'realities' of the military-industrial complex. When I suggested that the foes of the university are outside, not inside, he translated that statement into the crude notion that I meant the trustees were invading curricula." Two weeks later the radical students, inflamed by Pusey's procrastination, occupied University Hall.

Pusey drew the heaviest fire for calling the police. But in

actuality, most university presidents hide authoritarian tendencies behind their florid rhetoric. No matter how skillful a negotiator, moral philosopher or lawyer he may be, a president committed to "harmonizing" the existing institution will encounter opposition from students. And when he does, his gut reaction is to strike back, even if he doesn't call police. The University of Chicago's president, Edward Levi, is a good case in point. Although he did not summon police during the fourteen-day occupation of the administration building in February, 1969, he adopted the rigid administrative posture that is bound to spell future violence. During the sit-in, Levi refused to negotiate with radicals, a position actually more intransigent than that of San Francisco State's S. I. Hayakawa.

The sit-in at Chicago started when the university announced it would not reappoint radical professor Marlene Dixon. Mrs. Dixon held a joint appointment with the Department of Sociology and the Committee on Human Development. The former unanimously recommended that she not be rehired; the latter voted unanimously the opposite way. In a similar "split" recommendation case a year earlier, Levi (then provost) had forced two divided forces to resolve the conflict themselves. In the Dixon case, Levi's successor simply accepted the split recommendation, which was tantamount to firing her.

In view of the fact that Mrs. Dixon's salary was paid by the Human Development group that wanted her back, a compromise might have been possible. Instead Levi backed the idea of a special investigatory panel and retreated from sight behind the skirts of his faculty, which was turning out a daily torrent of support through the press information office. Despite several overtures from students for a tiny concession that could start the talks to bring them out of the occupied building, he refused to permit any discussion that smacked of negotiation. He even refused to discuss the matter with his special students' advisory group. He also refused to call the police, because they might have broken the psychological hammer lock the faculty had on the students sitting in. The administrative temperature was running very high, however. At one point, a vice-president, fearing his files had been rifled, charged into the occupied building and almost engaged in fisticuffs with an innocent bystander.

To the press and the world, Levi's handling of the situation seemed a superb testimony to reasoned administration. After the sit-in collapsed, he reappeared with a statement praising his handling of the demonstration. "In a world of considerable violence," he said, "the university has emphasized the persuasive power of ideas." In fact, however, the power of ideas, as represented by the radical Mrs. Dixon and the Committee on Human Development, has been squashed by the well-entrenched sociology department and the machinery of the administration. In the aftermath of the crisis, disciplinary committees began processing the cases of eighty-two students who participated in the sit-in. When a small, angry student mob staged a later protest at Levi's house, causing slight damage, the president took off the velvet gloves. Henceforth, a dean announced, the university would not "hesitate to call in police if disruptions occur." A few weeks later some forty Chicago students were suspended in one of the strongest disciplinary actions of the year at any school.

The president of a private university punishes radical students because in the recesses of his mind he believes they are the discordant note in an otherwise perfect harmony. The president of a large public university has no illusions of har-

mony. He knows that as a practical matter, if student enroll-
ments help build buildings, students in the flesh can destroy
financial support. The multi-campus state institutions have
been especially susceptible to public pressure because they are
in a period of rapid growth. "Among 9 institutions in 1960,"
says a University of Alabama lobbyist, "we were the un-
questioned leaders. Among 30 today we really have to scrap.
That's why we worry the students will jeopardize our chances:
we're always hearing complaints about radicals and beatniks
in the cloakrooms. We don't want to crush student initiative,
we just have to keep the larger value focus in mind. I want to
be brave. I want to step out. I want to say the students have
complete freedom. But as a financial man I have to ask myself: is this the right step at the right time?"

Even as the new buildings go up, pandering to the public
has many disadvantages, which make themselves felt later.
For one thing, public relations gimmicks, such as football,
become more important than education. At Alabama, football coach Paul "Bear" Bryant is probably more influential
both inside and outside the institution, than President Frank
Rose. When Afro-American Society leaders complained to
the administration about Bryant's all-white football teams, a
top vice-president said sadly, "We need your help. I tried to
talk to the Bear once on this, but it didn't do any good."

The sad irony about football is that its backers are like
Mafia drug czars in the ghetto. They get students so strung
out on the need for competitive sports to break up the daily
monotony that they will enthusiastically approve the use of
student fees to support an already lucrative enterprise. But
the most exploited "junkies" in this process are the athletes.
They are encouraged to take specially-tailored mickey-mouse
courses so as not to jeopardize their athletic standing. At most

Big Ten schools, only a small percentage of the eagerly-recruited black athletes graduate. If they can't go on to professional teams, they then face lives as physical education instructors or sports bums with trophy-filled attics.

The students are also shills for financing the expansion of large multi-campus state universities. A financial vice-president of a Midwestern state multiversity explains:

"If we didn't grow we'd die. The economics of higher education demand that you grow constantly as a budgetary weapon. The principle is simply this: you get more money for more students which can be applied to programs elsewhere. Even legislators on a cost-cutting binge will hesitate to cut back the current level of appropriations per student. In other words, if you've established in the previous budget that it costs $1,000 to educate one sophomore and you can show that there will be 25 new sophomores in the next class then the legislature will give you $25,000 practically without question. That extra 25 grand, however, is not necessarily applied to those sophomores: rather, you may use it to pay the salary for an atomic energy professor who may have only 10 special graduate students."

The vice-president, speaking off-the-record, pauses for breath and adds, "The dynamics of higher education require that you're always wheeling and dealing because the men in the capitol are not educators, they're insurance salesmen or lawyers or businessmen—people who like to work with figures. Thus, we give them plenty of formulas. When one doesn't work in our favor we invent another one." The so-called dynamics of growth also mean that campuses become larger and larger and much less manageable. But that doesn't seem to bother this man. He frankly says, "The student management problems will be the same whether you have 10,000 or 50,000 students. You just have to be careful that not more than a few percent of those students get up in arms at one time."

The real problem is not controlling the students but holding back the tide of public antagonism unleashed by any sort of protest. This is the penalty for all those years of florid Rotary Club speeches in which presidents have wooed citizens on how old Multi-U benefits the public. As University of Texas President Norman Hackerman explains, "We've been linking education to the welfare of citizens for so long, that we've gotten people almost too interested. Nowadays, when a citizen rides on rough roads, he takes issue with the highway commission. When a protest occurs, he looks to the president to steamroller the bumps."

Therefore in times of crisis a president finds that the only way he can answer the legitimate grievances of students is to crack their heads. He can't blame the faculty for neglecting students. After all, he's a faculty man who serves at the pleasure of the faculty. He can't blame the public for creating a repressive political climate. They control his budget and can create more repressive rules any time they feel like it. Obviously he can't blame himself. So that leaves only one scapegoat—the students. And whether the students are right or wrong on any given issue is irrelevant. They must lose simply because they are students.

A tale of three chancellors at the University of Wisconsin shows this best. Over a period of three years (1967–1969) the Madison chancellorship has become roughly equivalent to the job of police dispatcher. In February of 1967, Madison students blocked Dow Chemical Company recruiters. A small group of protestors was arrested and jailed. Chancellor Fleming realized that since the police had jailed all the "leaders" of the uprising, there was no one on the outside to call off the continuing demonstrations. So he went to the jailhouse and freed the only people who could shut off further trouble. To do so, he personally wrote a check for $1,200 bond. He was widely hailed in liberal academic circles for having shown sympathy to dissidents under fire—in great part, because this piece of showmanship calmed the campus. Shortly thereafter he was offered the presidency of two Big-Ten universities. In fact, he explained to the conservative University of Michigan regents, who eventually hired him as president in 1967, that the bail check had been a tactic to restore order.

When Fleming went on to the Michigan presidency, his Wisconsin friends joked that he "got out of town one step ahead of the police." His successor, sociologist William Sewell, didn't. Sewell was opposed to the idea of using force, yet eventually buckled under to advisors, who warned that a stern posture before the fact could head off trouble. During the weeks when the antiwar forces were gathering momentum for another demonstration against Dow in fall, 1967, the Dean of Student's Office issued strident warnings against any attempts at disruption. When the students began a sit-in that tied up part of Bascom Hall, the police were already visible in the parking lot. The students, stirred up by this sight, refused to be carried out peacefully, as they had originally intended. The police conducted a medieval charge, pummeling everything in their way. The resulting brutality weighed heavily on Sewell. "He was a typical sociologist," a central administration official fumed. "He wanted to take time out and study the root causes." In June, 1968, he took a leave of absence from the university for a year.

The final leg on the tripod was Edwin Young, a long-time

faculty member of the University of Maine who had been getting seasoning as its president. A tough New Englander, he believed that everybody should act respectably and behave decently toward one another. However, he shared the no-nonsense approach favored by the central administration. "The lesson of Dow," said presidential aide Robert Taylor, "was that you don't try to handle these things with too little, too late." One of Young's first assignments as Wisconsin's chancellor was to build up better liaison with the Madison and the county police. "It's amazing how those guys respond when you show a little trust and respect for them," said Taylor. "They were really helpful. For example, we don't have any student informants. They have dirty and bearded police working on campus who do undercover work, mostly on drugs. These guys were a tremendous cross-check on our own student affairs people, who had not been very good intelligence sources in the past. In January and early February, we were getting undercover information that black and white radicals were meeting—so we knew what was brewing."

Within minutes after a student rally had decided on a Saturday morning to disrupt a basketball game that afternoon, the Wisconsin Mod Squad was relaying the word back to police headquarters. The Madison police arrived at the field house long before the students could get there. Back at the administration building, Robert Taylor, representing the president, who was in the East, Chancellor Young, and student-affairs aides were setting up a command post. The early arrival of the police kept most of the radical students out of the building. Nevertheless, Governor Warren Knowles' limousine was scratched and its license plate stolen while he was inside watching the game. Getting word of the damage on his hotline long before anyone inside knew about it,

Taylor paged a university official at the field house and asked him to tell the governor. Forewarned, the governor walked out calm and smiling and got into an unmarked car. "Our work was so effective," Taylor bragged, "that we knew more about what was really happening at that game than the broadcasters."

The hard-line administration tactics continued throughout the week of the strike at Wisconsin. Almost from the beginning, the command team included a representative of the Adjutant General, who was in charge of the National Guard troops. At midweek, when the police were obviously tiring, the governor called for troops, and some 2,000 previously alerted National Guardsmen arrived within three hours. "Calling out the Guard was a very popular move," said Taylor. "They also had a very calming effect on the campus. Many of them were young and cherubic and looked like students." To keep the Guardsmen from cracking under the strain, they were afforded a full recreational program during off-duty hours, which included swimming and basketball in the gym where they were stationed. However, the captain did make one very unpopular rule: he forbade his young troops to talk to girls.

After the strike had been tidied up, the university now turned energetically to the problem of disciplinary action. Despite the fact that the regents had personally supervised the revision of a student-discipline code with heavy penalties against obstruction, the code was rendered obsolete by student tactics. As Robert Taylor explained, "The principle of their cat-and-mouse games was don't do anything that the police can get you on. They were thus able to break the rules and not get caught. There were only about 40 arrests altogether during the entire week. We didn't have a rule, for instance, which would protect administrators from abuse. A kid could call the president a 'dirty mother-fucker' and he might get a $25 fine in municipal court for misconduct. But we couldn't touch him."

The regents also felt that the due-process protections written into the code were used to coddle student criminals. "One problem with due process," said Taylor, "is that it's like when a puppy makes no-no in the corner. When you rub his nose in it a day later, he doesn't remember the offense. Because we weren't able to punish violators right away, they could continue to incite others without any check." A week after the strike ended, a foolish group of students smashed windows and damaged property in Bascom Hall. This was clearly an isolated post-strike spasm that did not threaten to incite further violence. But the regents, looking angrily for scapegoats, threw three of the students out of school without a hearing on the recommendation of the chancellor and president.

For his general handling of the strike, Chancellor Young became an instant hero in Wisconsin. But he did not relish much of the fan mail linking his name with that of another newborn national figure, S. I. Hayakawa.

In contrast to such long-established citadels as Harvard and Wisconsin, the University of California at Berkeley has gained stature only since World War II. However, in terms of the rapidly-evolving protest scene, Berkeley has become a veritable Williamsburg. In four years of turbulence, nothing has really changed. All the historic monuments and sites have been preserved. Each day tourists pour out of the Grey Line buses and flock to noon protest rallies where they shoot the action, just like the police photographers. Sproul Hall still reeks of tear gas, and Wheeler Auditorium has been recently gutted by fire. Windows of the chancellor's office in Dwinelle Hall are still boarded up.

Inside Dwinelle Hall is perhaps the most undaunted monument at Berkeley—Roger W. Heyns. The chancellor's hair is grayer, his ties are wider, and his manner unabashed after four years of continuous turmoil. "I like administration and I'm good at it," he says brashly. "I'm not one of those weeping violets talking about getting back to a scholarly career." Yet he concedes that a smaller school, with a less abrasive atmosphere, would be more suited to his small-town sensibilities. He was born in Grand Rapids, Michigan and attended nearby Hope and Calvin Colleges before journeying to the big city, Ann Arbor, to win fame and fortune. As a psychology professor, dean, and then vice-president at Michigan, he always managed to be both an innovator and popular with everyone. In the early sixties, he lent his name and energy to the most imaginative proposals, such as equal-educational-opportunity programs and residential mini-colleges within the multiversity. At the same time he was a great believer in working through channels. He was fond of saying "it is easier to move a cemetery than change a curriculum"— and he had the patience and tenacity to push, headstone by headstone.

Like so many prestigious educators of the early sixties, Heyns essentially has the mediator's simplistic, and sometimes nostalgic view of the university as a community pushing and plugging together. At one of his first Berkeley convocations in 1965, Heyns rallied the band to strike up the school song, but no one knew the words. His earliest visions of reforms were likewise sentimental, more suited to an intimate liberal arts faculty, which generally has some feeling for undergraduate education, than to a multiversity. As Charles

Muscatine, the medieval English scholar, complained: "His idea of reform was to push for a department of religious studies. But that idea has been tried for 2000 years." Furthermore, Heyns was less at home with some of the famed Muscatine Committee's more radical proposals, such as vastly broadened off-campus study.

As an administrator, Heyns refused to decentralize. "If I say that I am going to delegate," he explains, "then the principles of social psychology and morality mean I must delegate. I can't be a monitor making a decison-by-decision review. I realized from the beginning that the regents were clearly holding me responsible for all student activities. So in order to delegate, I had to have an apparatus which would guarantee responsibility and moderation. Given the influence of radicals in most campus groups, such confidence was impossible."

The principles of social psychology also dictated that he reel back the slack in the lines to the student government. In November of 1967 Heyns placed the entire student-union complex, previously controlled by the students, in the hands of an adult-dominated program-and-facilities board. He was ostensibly retaliating for the fact that graduate students had been allowed to vote in campus elections that week. Actually, he was angered that the student government had been trying to cut back funds for the band and choir in order to sponsor community-action programs. "We are not going to turn this school into a political playground," he thundered. "The band and choir people are genuinely interested in their activity. They don't want to be politicians to protect it."

The reason for this tight-reined style was his obsession with peace-at-any-price. In his first major address to the academic senate in 1965, Heyns declared, "The relevant categories for us must not be what is lawful or unlawful, but what are the interests of the University community which must be protected by University rules." In a school already polarized—by the administration's extreme rigidity and its contradictory disregard for students' constitutional rights— this was the worst possible approach. Thereafter, Heyns made the final decisions on rules, Heyns made the final decisions on disciplinary penalties, Heyns made the final decisions on which activities were "political" and which were "educational." In the process of disciplining over 400 students in the past four years, Heyns radicalized thousands.

A typical example of Heyn's approach occurred during "Stop The Draft Week" in October, 1967. Originally Heyns had promised that the students could have a teach-in, but backed off in the face of a county court injunction banning advocacy of off-campus political activity. The students, naturally, were bitter that the university didn't contest the obvious illegality of the injunction. So they went ahead and held a series of rallies violating the campus rules governing time, place, and manner. Heyns suspended two students and the dean of students reprimanded sixty-two others. Then 1,000 demonstrators staged a mill-in that tied up Sproul Hall for three days, in protest of the suspensions. Heyns added four more suspensions and twenty-eight reprimands to his list. Furthermore, some of the probationary reprimands banned students from being "active members" in student organizations, although they could still go to class or use the health center. One sophomore had to register at the dean's office as a "non-student speaker" every time he wanted to attend an SDS meeting. His probationary terms were so complicated that he would carry them around like a contract to iron out disputes with deans over what he could and could not do.

Heyns, of course, liked to portray himself as a hapless middleman being victimized by steadily-escalating attacks from left and right. He assumed, like a Kerr mediator-initiator, that there is a rational center ground. But the Cleaver controversy in the fall of 1968 proved that a search for coherence within the multiversity was futile.

Having failed to head off the Cleaver case before it became a public spectacle, he bounced back and forth, like a Ping-Pong ball, urging moderation on all sides. He asked the regents, who allotted Cleaver only one appearance to present his case, to support Cleaver's course. He then asked the four faculty sponsors to postpone the course for one quarter. They refused. In desperation, he made a room available for a non-credit course, but the students still staged two sit-ins, demanding that the course be granted credit. And finally, Heyns also went before the academic senate to recommend that it not provoke further confrontation by vowing implacably to give credit for the course. "In the matter of courses," he said humbly, "the chancellor stands on the sidelines. If he is summoned to participate—or, I should say, when he is summoned to account for the acts of others—it is late in the game. The shadows on the field are long and the crowd around the goal posts restive." Then, describing his failure at all points, he added, "Armed with this record as an advisor, I enter this matter once again, this time because of my belief that in the restive crowd I mentioned earlier there are people who want to tear down much more than the goal posts." At last he found sympathy. The faculty condemned the regents for their "hasty and ill-timed action." But they did nothing. Heyns' final view was that "while I got everybody in the place mad at me, I avoided total disaster."

Not really, for the Cleaver crisis was slowly generating

into the more explosive issue of the black college. To be sure, the black students themselves were angrier with Cleaver for not involving them in his course than they were with the administration. But their own demand for a black studies department was not moving along fast enough. They had originally suggested it in June, 1968. Heyns had appointed a black sociologist to come up with a detailed proposal and then tried to nudge the recommended department through faculty channels. As usual, it got stuck going through an executive committee in January, 1969.

By the time the committee accepted the concept of a black department, and three faculty senate committees concurred on it in a record forty-eight hours, the militant Third World Liberation Front had called a strike. From that point on, the scenario was all too familiar. As Heyns desperately dangled the latest faculty offer before the outraged students, they produced picket signs calling for an autonomous Ethnic College. The ensuing strike was supported by thousands of marchers in serpentine lines. Heyns asked Governor Reagan for highway patrolmen, and Reagan turned the request into an "Emergency Proclamation." For several weeks in February, the students and cops squared off daily before a national television audience.

Eventually, as the winter quarter ended and calm was miraculously restored, Heyns raised the ante. He said he would establish an ethnic department under his office, which would develop into a college. The faculty thought this was a fine idea. The students rather glumly accepted it, since, as they pointed out, a college under the chancellor was not likely to be very autonomous. Heyns stoically insisted that his intentions were good. The campus simmered.

When the new quarter began in April, the action switched

to the streets. So-called "street people" and students voluntarily transformed a vacant, off-campus lot belonging to the university into a "People's Park," with sod, swing sets, and small trees. After a few weeks, Berkeley Councilman John Debonis and other local residents complained about the park in a letter to the UC regents. Heyns was not anxious to jump into another fray, for he was naturally sensitive to the needs of the community. As he once told a *Time* reporter, "The university of the sixties is a city, and the problem is how to get neighborhoods within that city, otherwise you have loneliness and anonymity." As a university administrator, though, he finally felt obliged to send in the police at 5 A.M., May 16, to evict the street people. The police were followed by construction crews, who surrounded the 270-by-450-foot lot with an eight-foot-high fence in six hours flat. Perhaps sensing the next act, Heyns promptly left for Washington and his executive vice-chancellor for Los Angeles.

After a noon rally, hundreds of Berkeley students marched on the park at the urging of the president-elect of the student body. On the way they met Alameda County sheriffs, who proceeded to kill one youth, blind another, and wound at least thirty others with buckshot at point-blank range. In Sacramento, Ronald Reagan and his education advisor Alex Sheriffs (formerly a hard-line Berkeley vice-chancellor who helped touch off the FSM debacle in 1964) quickly arranged for 2,000 National Guardsmen to move into Berkeley. The move was expedited by the fact that the governor had never lifted the "State of Extreme Emergency" imposed during the Third World strike. For the next week it was open season on Berkeley students. As National Guardsmen bivouacked in "People's Park," helicopters dusted the verdant campus with nauseating CS gas and the police defended the university's property rights. As students marched around town planting flowers and shrubbery, police quickly moved in and seized the greenery. "Go limp, go limp," screamed the students as the police tossed the vegetation into their paddy wagons.

On May 22 the police and guardsmen swept 482 protestors, shoppers, reporters, and one mailman into the Bank of America parking lot in downtown Berkeley. They were bussed to the Alameda County Jail, which had jocularly become known as the "Santa Rita campus." There they were so badly roughed up by prison officials that the district court issued an order restraining the sheriff's deputies from beating up the prisoners. Sheriff Frank Madigan apologized, explaining that many of his deputies were young Viet Nam veterans and "they take a very dim view of this situation. . . . They having a feeling that these prisoners should be treated like Viet Cong. But subsequently, charges were dropped against all persons arrested during the May 22 police sweep.

Finally, as thousands of sympathizers prepared to march on Memorial Day, Heyns came out in favor of leasing the eastern portion of the lot to the city. But he insisted that the fence should not come down, lest it jeopardize what he called "delicate discussions." Governor Reagan subsequently withdrew the National Guardsmen, while Heyns took some attention off the park by turning over the records of more than 300 students and eleven student organizations to the McClellan committee (the Senate Permanent Sub-Committee on Investigations). And with that, the curtain came down on another term at Berkeley. (During the summer of 1969, the Regents voted to divide the People's Park site into a parking lot and soccer field.)

Roger Heyns seemed relatively serene at the end of his

fourth year in the Berkeley chancellor's office. As the author of *The Psychology of Personal Adjustment,* he had long understood the inevitability of change, even in himself. "The adjustment of people in their forties, fifties and sixties is complicated . . . by changes in abilities . . . and by the inse- cure vocational situation. . . . These changes are threats to the security and well-being of older people. Many of the negative traits attributed to them—such as stubbornness, in- flexibility, and the tendency to be opinionated and dogmatic —can be understood as responses to these threats."

# CHAPTER 4:

# BLACK STUDIES

**H**enry Rosovsky just can't win. An economist and a specialist in the Japanese development since the Meiji restoration, he has been sought by and served in the top universities in the country. But the student rebellion has upset his professional life. After the FSM erupted in 1964, he sold his large house in the Berkeley hills; he moved to Harvard the following year, hoping to find quietude by the Charles River. "When I left California," he sighs, "I thought that student power might be a local Berkeley phenomenon." At Harvard he enjoyed three years of peace before he was sucked in by the maelstrom again. In May of 1968 he accepted the chairmanship of The Faculty Committee on African and Afro-American studies. As a social scientist interested in generating new academic currents, he wanted to see "whether Afro-American studies really was a discipline."

Eight months later his committee concluded that it was. The committee's report said, "It can hardly be doubted that the study of black men in America is a legitimate and urgent academic endeavor." Approved by the arts and sciences faculty in February of 1969, the report was seen as a significant event in higher education, because it placed Harvard's exclusive sanction on a pioneer field. The Rosovsky report committed Harvard to a degree-granting program in Afro-American studies, which would be implemented by a second Standing Faculty Committee using students as advisors in recruiting personnel.[1]

Of course the over-all faculty would still oversee the program. "No recommendations have been made," Rosovsky told his colleagues, "which in any way go counter to our long-established review procedures or lines of authority." But

[1]For those professors and administrators in the reading audience who like to use Harvard as a do-it-yourself kit for their own restructuring gambits, we will give footnotes on the juicy details of the various black studies plans as they evolved. For those students tired of restructuring proposals and interested in actual reforms, we suggest you stay with the main text. You can supply the details from your own schools.

The Rosovsky report was a typical liberal faculty document, willing to recognize the need for "greater emphasis on the experience of Afro-Americans in courses," but unwilling to allow too much latitude to blacks in running their own program. The plan called for a Standing Faculty Committee on Afro-American Studies, whose first major black appointee would become the minority-of-one chairman. The relationship of black students to the committee was more vague. They would be part of a subsidiary personnel panel. The main Committee, absorbing the new black scholars might, "for certain particular purposes," add student voting members. Since even the black faculty would be outnumbered, the black students could hardly be expected to cool their heels until their presence suited the "particular purposes" of the committee. In short, as a working document for future growth, the Rosovsky plan was doomed to failure from the beginning.

Rosovsky himself felt concerned that black students, who supported the report as consultants, would later demand a greater participatory voice. "I was a superb diplomat," he confesses modestly. "I made every effort possible to lock in the moderate black students to the plan so that they wouldn't renege later."

Although he was appointed to the new Standing Committee implementing black studies, Rosovsky's diplomatic victory lasted only two months. On April 7, 1969, two days before white students were to occupy University Hall over the ROTC issue, the committee issued a communique for potential concentrators in black studies that black studies courses could not serve as a full major, but would require a second field of concentration. The committee felt it was only a minor, temporary decision, easily revocable later. The black students, who had not been consulted on this matter, saw it as a dangerous trend. "The promises of winter," they declared, "have given way to the putrescence of spring." Buoyed by the SDS strike, and angered by the fact that three "brothers" outside the building had been clubbed during the police bust, they demanded that the committee be dissolved and replaced by a new governing body which would include them as full voting members. When the faculty eventually added six black students to the seven-man committee, Rosovsky resigned. As he explained later, "I honestly don't feel that black students are qualified to set up an academic program at Harvard just because they have soul."

Nor was Rosovsky alone in his consternation. The confusion surrounding the faculty vote, and the sour-graping afterwards, indicated that the Harvard faculty was a long way from being committed to black studies as the students envisioned them. The vote, in fact, has to be understood in the chaotic context of other events at Harvard and elsewhere. After the sit-in and police bust, the faculty's foremost concerns were the University Hall issues, particularly reaffirmation of its anti-ROTC stand. So the black demands for greater participation were held over until April 22. By then the "conservative" and "liberal" caucuses, which guide the general faculty assembly, had met for a long weekend of feverish negotiations on the black questions. The fever was intensified by the fact that on Sunday, April 20 the black students at Cornell were photographed leaving the union with guns and bandoliers. The conservative caucus, the dean, and some members of the liberal caucus agreed to support a resolution by sociologist Alex Inkeles. His plan promised departmental status to black studies and offered students a voting participation in choosing new faculty. However, the students would have no guarantee of voting privileges once the department was officially established. Since the students were already personnel advisors, they labeled Inkeles plan "Rosovsky with cream and sugar."[2]

[2]Inkeles did consult black students, but his plan reeked of manipulation. In brief, he would have given students voting membership on the Standing Committee. Then he stripped that committee of its personnel function and set up an Extraordinary Commission for appointments purposes, on which students would be a decided minority. As in Rosovsky's plan, they would still have no defined participation once the real department was set up. Now, for all the chilling details.

The Standing Committee would be expanded to include six students—three chosen by the Afro, three chosen by potential concentrators. Then this Standing Committee would be downgraded in importance and stripped of its appointment power. To facilitate appointments, the president would create an Extraordinary Commission with three faculty members, three "distinguished leaders of the black community, at least two holding academic appointments," and three black students. This Commission would exist until four new faculty members, including at least two with tenure, had arrived in Cambridge. They would then form an Executive Committee, which "in consultation with the interested students" would propose a temporary charter for their operations to the faculty. In 1972, a permanent constitution would be proposed.

The black students devised a clever strategy using the Inkeles plan. They saw in certain passages, such as the florid introductory sentence,[3] a perfect adornment for their own proposal that black students be included, in just about equal proportions to faculty members on all committees making decisions currently and in the future. Thus they used Inkeles' motion as a Trojan horse to catch the faculty off guard. The strategy worked to perfection. The assembly chairman, Dean Edward Mason, had decided that given the emotionality of the times, he should allow Afro—the black student organization—to present their motion directly so that it could be voted up or down. After consulting with both caucuses, Mason felt confident the motion would be voted down and the Inkeles proposal accepted. But the strategy backfired. The blacks were invited to the meeting. They waved their academically-scented motion with one hand and made a fist with the other; the faculty, alternately thrilled and cowed, adopted the Afro motion with some minor changes. The Inkeles motion never came to the floor. The historians, economists, and sociologists who had led the fight against Afro

---

Again, one can see the academic mind neatly playing word games, but making little real structural change. Students would, by virtue of their seats on the Standing Committee, be involved in overseeing "expansion of library resources," soliciting funds for department chairs, and developing an Afro-American Research Institute. But the important task of selecting faculty would be placed in the hands of a commission appointed by Nathan Pusey which would, of course, be heavily weighted toward the faculty point of view. As the crowning insult, the black students would have no guarantee that the new black scholars, once they arrived, would be given official voting status in the new department. The effect of the Inkeles plan would be to give the black faculty members eventual control of their own department, but they would still have to be constitutionally accredited by the faculty as a whole. The whole scheme is like a British plan for allowing some 99-percent-illiterate colony to gradually assume home rule under the watchful eye of the Queen Mother.

[3]Lifting Inkeles' first sentence exactly, "the Faculty intends The Afro-

naturally screamed "Munich." "What most other universities have bled and died over," cried one, "Harvard gave up for nothing."

But the most persistent faculty reaction was confusion. Inkeles, ever the behaviorist, reported with disgust, "I asked twenty people in a row why they voted the way they did— and not one of them could give me a coherent answer. Of course, maybe I had a bad sampling." Fortunately, other social scientists retained their 20–20 academic vision. Seymour Martin Lipset, the specialist on student politics, speculated that the fault lay in breaking tradititon by letting students speak directly to the faculty, often in rebuttal. "When you admit students to the discussion, the issue naturally gravitates to their level. In addition, when people with different viewpoints have a face-to-face dialogue, the tendency is to soften opposition and bring about conciliation. These are very dangerous procedures for a faculty trying to preserve its own independence. After all, the theory behind separate legislative estates is to give men a chance to freely vote their own prejudices in their own assemblies."

Others seemed to agree that there had been procedural

---

American Studies Program to be a department, interdisciplinary in nature, offering a standard field of concentration." The Afro proposal continued, in style and organization, to look like a copy of the Inkeles proposal, setting up a Standing Committee that would oversee library expansion and solicit funds for departmental chairs. However, the blacks made some subtle but significant changes. For example, where Inkeles had given power of appointment to the Extraordinary Commission, the blacks had the Standing Committee nominate the first four to six members. Then, where Inkeles eventually turned the power over to the newly-appointed faculty in an executive committee without students, the black students provided for equal membership. Those two simple changes made all the difference. But the marvel of the Afro proposal was that you would really have to study it for a few minutes to realize that it was not Inkeles' proposal. This proves that both sides can play the liberal-rhetoric game, yet be on opposite sides of the fence.

breakdowns. Robert McCloskey, the government chairman and leader of the conservative caucus, felt the liberal caucus leaders had failed to keep their members in line. "Pardon the expression," he snorted, "but their caucus is like an SDS meeting; people wander in and out, and whoever is there, even the wives, may vote." Sociologist Talcott Parsons viewed the defeat in nondemocratic terms. "The Communist Party may be able to sit through four- and six-hour meetings," he thumped on his desk; "but not the Harvard faculty."

Only the experimental scientists, staunch supporters of the Afro plan, seemed to believe in the powers of youth. Psychologist Jerome Bruner, noting the "dyspeptic bad humor" of certain social scientists, gave a strong endorsement to the students as spear-carriers for the new technology. "I'll take you up to the computer lab, and you won't find anyone over twenty-five doing anything interesting. I'm no fool, but when I'm running my experiments on sucking patterns, I take my programs up there where some paternalistic 19- or 20-year-old debugs it for me. Yes, we're very used to young people being smart around here." J. D. Watson, the Nobel laureate who discovered DNA structure at Cambridge, noted that if he and Francis Crick (who had no doctorate) had listened to their elders, the discovery of the double helix might have been delayed. "In a new field," he explained, "age can be a handicap. I would rather have a young brilliant black like Eldridge Cleaver jutting off in different directions than some tame Negro economist who will just set up another economics department."[4]

The administration, however, did not share Watson's en-

[4]Even after discovering DNA, the precocious Watson encountered some difficulty from his elders. When he submitted his personal and highly-readable account of the discovery, *The Double Helix,* to the Harvard Uni-

thusiasm. President Pusey, the man too busy to talk to radicals because he was working on faculty appointments, cast a dubious eye at the faculty antics. "Many faculty members simply aren't equipped to make instant decisions. They may never come out of a lab or spend all their time working with insects in a museum or writing reports in the bowels of a library. They're the kind of human beings who never participate in any group activity; their value lies elsewhere." Meanwhile, Acting Dean Edward S. Mason, stunned and alarmed by the behavior of the faculty committee, prepared a memo for Dean Franklin Ford, who had been side-lined by a stroke. "I want to prepare the Dean's office for more thorough scrutiny of every recommendation that comes from that committee. No recommendations will be accepted unless they are unanimous."

For the time being, all seemed calm. The standing committee, which had created a search committee under Talcott Parsons, reached unanimity in its choices for the new black studies department. However, their early choices—Chicago's John Hope Franklin, Stanford's Saint Clair Drake, and Harvard's own Martin Kilson—declined appoointment, and the faculty fretted that even Harvard's name couldn't lure top scholars to a department with student participants. At the end of the year, the search committee was still searching, and Henry Rosovsky had gone back to the Meiji restoration. Harvard was peaceful again. Rosovsky could get some satisfaction from an administrator who assured him, "Why are you so pessimistic? In a year the faculty will turn conservative and everything will be back under control."

versity Press, its publication was blocked by Pusey on the grounds that it was "inappropriate." The book was published by an established commercial publisher, won critical acclaim, and became a best seller.

The conflict between strident students and defensive faculty echoes through the academic world. But the conflict over black studies seems to be a distinct one, and a harbinger of the rapid transition that universities and their denizens must undergo. Where the traditional professor, with his Ph.D. as his Bible, has been a missionary to the unwashed, the black professor will be prized for experiential as well as academic credentials. Where the traditional curriculum has been a way station for the upwardly mobile on their way to the suburbs, the future black curriculum will cultivate intellects and attitudes that will guide the graduate back to his native home. Where the traditional university has been aloof from messy community involvements that restrict intellectual freedom, the black studies program will renew the land-grant spirit in an urban setting. And finally, where traditional academic programs have emphasized continuity and stability, black studies will make sudden jags as experience warrants. As one Harvard black student, wary of academic inertia, put it, "We want a program that can bend to accommodate the aspirations of brothers still in the cradle."

The Harvard black studies program, drawing a middle-class black student into an elitist institution with departmental structures like the Army's,[5] can hardly be expected to be as innovative as the modern urban world warrants. So even the black students were willing to hire a traditional Ne-

[5]The generals in this case are the tenured faculty with plush corner offices and secretaries. The privates are the assistant professors, whose accommodations sometimes resemble the slave quarters of teaching assistants at most schools. The division in rank is accentuated by the fact that in a department like economics, with twenty-five assistant professors, only one or two will be granted tenure. The others are expected to go elsewhere for seasoning and then, when they are clearly rocketing toward fame, implore Harvard to hire them back.

gro scholar, at a time when young blacks across the country were combing the movement and black writers' colonies for talent. One graduating black senior, a brilliant and articulate student, said with disdain of San Francisco State's Nathan Hare, "The trouble with Nathan Hare is that he's not too bright."

The hope for a truly urban university would seem to lie, therefore, in a school like Washington's Federal City College, which opened for the 1968–69 academic year. The nation's first "urban-grant" university (chartered under the Morrill Act), Federal City is located in America's most desolate colony, the District of Columbia. The name "City College," and its temporary campus in the former SEC building might suggest a second-rate institution like dozens of other new colleges opening every year. But that's not the case at all. Federal City College represented a jewel in the mind's eye of liberal Washingtonians, who saw the college as a first-rate public university, and citadel in the struggle for home rule.

In fact, many distinguished scholars were attracted by its promise. "Washington offered a frontier situation with all the comforts of home," rhapsodized Kenneth Lynn, the American-studies scholar from Harvard, who was wooed over cocktails at the exclusive Recess Club. Along with many of the idealistic whites who joined the faculty, Lynn saw Federal City College as "the fulfillment of a national dream going back to George Washington, a school for the District of Columbia community yet every bit as good as a top-flight state university with a sizeable out-of-state enrollment." Al Lefcowicz, an English professor from Howard, "thought we could supply an experimental quality education as good as Harvard or Amherst, even if it took more than four years for some students." Donal Jones, an avid supporter of the San

Francisco State experimental college, "picked up the newspaper, read about Federal City College, called the president
and went to work for him five days later." Others hastily
bailed out of other commitments to come aboard early in
1968 for planning purposes. Describing some of these eager
tigers, faculty chairman Joe Brent said, "If you put this faculty at San Francisco State, it would be out running guns
for the Panthers."

Despite their zeal, something was missing. As Donal Jones
put it, "The school was too pasteurized, too sterile, more like
a McCarthy headquarters than an institution at the service
of the ghetto. The place needed blackening up a little." Nata-
lie Arrington, one of the few early Negro recruits recalled,
"We kept watching and waiting and wondering." Andress
Taylor, a black English professor from the South, was "re-
minded of the early phase of the civil rights movement; the
whites knew exactly what the blacks needed—a Harvard of
the slums." On June 1, when the whole faculty met for a
brief two-day convocation, the disparity was painfully evident: 70 percent of the faculty was white. As Taylor observed, "Since most of the faculty was white and most of the
janitors were black, we argued that the college needed more
white janitors and more black teachers. That's integration
mind you." In July he sponsored a resolution that affirmed
the faculty's desire to "hire blacks wherever possible" and
established a special committee that could recruit in the
South. When school opened in September, the balance was
nearly 50–50, and by September of 1969 it should easily be
70–30 the other way.

The most bitter racial battle was to be fought over the
curriculum. The administration, in its recruiting brochure,
set out a mouth-watering program of all the latest reforms—

core curriculum, interdisciplinary team teaching—plus all
the trimmings: small discussion groups, field trips, dramatic
readings, science labs with tapes and film strips so that "students proceed at their own pace rather than conducting the
set experiment of the day." Finally, a small, separate communications seminar would have students "giving class talks and
writing understandable reports."

They eventually developed such courses as "The Revolutionary Tradition" (beginning with Malcolm X or Cleaver
and dollying back through European and Third World revolutionary movements) and "Communication Arts" (ranging
across graphics, art, television, music, dramatic reading, and
communication theory).

Unfortunately, the interdisciplinary approach is an organizational as well as an educational method. Its success pre-
supposes the teamwork of lecturers and section and lab
readers. Such teamwork was impossible in a brand new
school in which many of the teachers didn't arrive until September and hammered out their reading lists the night before
classes began. Furthermore, while everyone agreed on a
broad, multidisciplinary approach in theory, there was almost
a childlike regression into the disciplinary womb when stress
developed. For example, an English professor would recommend that the entire first year be structured around writing.
The historians would insist that communication skills be integrated into the course "The Revolutionary Tradition."
When the faculty voted to follow the latter option, they
placed themselves in the ludicrous position of opening a
ghetto university without an English course, despite numerous students with reading and writing handicaps. Balance
was restored by the second quarter (January, 1969) when
the number of faculty members had been stabilized and stu-

dent wishes were better known. The number of courses quadrupled from 25 to 100 as interdisciplinary offerings were supplemented with such traditional courses as chemistry and English composition.

Not surprisingly, curriculum planning exacerbated racial tensions when the young blacks found themselves thwarted by smug, liberal professors cast in a new role as academic conservatives. Typically, at one faculty meeting an offended liberal, seeing his curriculum ideas scorned, declared, "If you want a school that promotes black pride, this is one thing. If you want a school that values knowledge and intellect, that's another." A black retorted, "The white teachers feel that because they deigned to give up their endowed chairs and come here, we should all kneel at their feet."

No one felt the pressure more than Provost David Dickson, a prominent Negro educator with recent experience as the "acknowledged Negro," to use his own phrase, in northern white universities. In October he made a public speech before a joint meeting of two major educational associations in which he described what he called the "racial tension, racial suspicion and racial polarization" threatening Federal City College. He added, "Our meetings display passion quite as much as reason, intimidation rather than discussion. The black and white moderates, shocked at the flight of sweet reason, are supine while the well-disciplined, intense cadre of white radicals and black separatists neglect academic principles for revolutionary ends." *The Washington Post* used the speech as a peg for a front-page story on racial tension at the school.

From his own point of view, Dickson may have been right to sound the alarm. In a city where a whisper of racial conflict is enough to send Southern congressmen into paroxysms of hysteria, the speech was a mistake. Dickson was also wrong in his assumptions. He was not describing Harvard, the mecca of Puritanism with 300 years of traditions, but Federal City College in its first year, with an integrated faculty in which both races were bound to be suffering a certain amount of culture shock.

It is true, of course, that the blacks had been challenging traditionalists like Dickson. But as Andress Taylor noted, "You can't set up a program to produce black militants any more than you can set one up not to produce them. Militancy is a function of social dynamics, not a curriculum. The curriculum only turns out X people with Y skills."

Actually, the young blacks had initially hoped that the whole curriculum might bear a "black" rather than "urban" orientation, so that there would be no need for a black studies program per se. But Jimmy Garrett, a twenty-six-year-old playwright and graduate of San Francisco State College (where he had organized the Black Students Union), swiftly recognized that given the political climate of the faculty, he would need a base. So he and a group of younger blacks began offering black studies courses in January, 1969. They also began formulating a master four-year program. The introduction to Garrett's program grandly declared, "If education is to be relevant to Black People, it must have a twofold purpose: revolution and nation-building."

The program was revolutionary, all right, but in an educational rather than a military sense. Its initial two years would be devoted to "decolonization of the mind" through intensive study of the African experience, and the last two years to "developing particular technical career skills"— again making heavy use of African materials. In addition, students would select from a wide range of languages, including Swahili, and discipline both mind and body with karate or stick fighting.

As the program began to take more definite shape, it became truly Afro-American, with more emphasis on the latter. Where traditional academic disciplines had been either theoretical (sociology) or practical (social work), black studies would unify the two. The study of architecture, for example, might range from environmental planning to bricklaying since blacks would have to confront urban planners as well as trade unions.

*The Washington Post* found the program both "revolutionary" and "separatist," as did many of the moderate teachers. But Garrett, supported by the student government, stuck to his guns. He pointed out that the program was "serious, concrete and systematic. It doesn't spend its time being anti-white." Indeed, as the year progressed, he showed a willingness to cross-breed with other divisions—the math department, for one, thus ending the hysteria about "black mathematics"—and to de-emphasize African study to allow students more flexibility. Meanwhile, blacks and whites throughout the college were getting over their culture shock, some through T-groups, most by the sensitivity therapy of faculty meetings. Provost Dickson would not accept the black studies program and resigned along with the president. The faculty, however, began rallying behind it. When the college's trustee board stopped hiring black studies personnel (because the program had not been approved), the faculty passed a unanimous censure for "discriminatory practice." The board recanted, and the faculty made plans to elect its own future provost.

Not all faculty members are happy with the new tone at Federal City. Kenneth Lynn, the school's highest paid, most prestigious scholar, will assume a new post at Johns Hopkins in the fall of 1969. "Unless intellectually respectable, black studies will represent another chapter in the self-delusion of the American Negro," he says. "Of course myth has a place in history. The writings of Frederick Jackson Turner are not invalidated by his theory of the frontier. But one can go too far. I expect Federal City will abolish the study of Marx next year because he was a European Jew; far better to contemplate Timbuktu in all its cultural glories."

The remaining blacks, who have brought so much vitality to the Harvard of the slums don't seem worried about his skepticism.

# CHAPTER 5

# THE URBAN UNIVERSITY

When thirty-six-year-old James M. Hester took over New York University in 1962, he found the school in an identity crisis. Like many urban universities, it was hard to locate. The buildings were scattered over various locations amid the city's concrete canyons. There were 43,000 students, most of them commuters who left the city after class. The main campus in Washington Square Park was and still is closer in spirit and geography to Fifth Avenue than to 125th Street.

As riots engulfed the nation in the middle sixties, Hester realized NYU could no longer be simply an educational sanctuary for rich kids who could afford $2,000 tuition. Urban blight was closing in on the entire city. No one was immune anymore. The problems of the tenements were also becoming the problems of the condominiums. The rats of Harlem were starting to show up on Park Avenue. The city's polluted air was plaguing everyone. Racial tensions threatened to overwhelm all New York.

President Hester believed that his university had an obligation, indeed a duty, to solve the urban crisis before it was too late. In order to establish NYU's new urban identity, Hester wanted a structural landmark that would put the school on the map. In 1967 he announced the construction of a twelve-story, $20,000,000 library that would be a beacon at Washington Square Park. "You can point at Harvard, you can point at Cornell, you can even point at Columbia, but you can't point at NYU," he declared.

The problem of developing psychological rapport with the community, particularly the black community, was also crucial in Hester's view. "In a country where higher education has been inclined to turn its face away from the city, where 'academic' still connotes an aloofness from political affairs, NYU is attuned to the people, the culture and the realities of urban life." The assassination of Martin Luther King in April of 1968 drove home those realities.

Like many self-conscious universities, NYU closed down for some soul searching, devoting an entire day to workshops on combating racism and increasing educational opportunities. Given a virtual carte blanche by the university, the school's 1,800 black students shaped a five-point program which would recruit minority students with a $1,000,000 scholarship fund, hire more black faculty, and establish a new Martin Luther King Afro-American Student Center, which would coordinate black cultural activities. The NYU administration enthusiastically accepted the program, and in July 1968 John Hatchett was hired to head the new black student center.

Hatchett, a former theology student, professor, and grade-school teacher, was hired on the recommendation of black students who knew him as a community leader. The thirty-eight-year-old Negro had not been impressed by NYU s initial effort to forge a new urban identity. He was one of many residents in the Washington Square Village apartment complex who had complained bitterly about the proposed NYU library eclipsing their precious sunlight.

The new, soft-spoken administrator was an unusual black revolutionary. As he liked to put it, "We are using the rhetoric of revolution, but all revolutions are not violent and all revolutions do not necessarily lead to violence." Instead, for American blacks emerging from domination by whites he advocated "psychological separation" rather than physical separation as the way to achieve personal identity. "Blackness," he believed, was "a state of mind to a large extent," and therefore even a black student in a white university could be unintegrated in the mental sense. "No black person in this country can find his identity and concomitantly pursue the goals of integration. Therefore some sort of separation is necessary. I have chosen to psychologically separate in order to get myself together."

Hatchett's views were not widely appreciated in New York, particularly in influential Jewish quarters. In February, 1968, Hatchett was fired for taking his PS 68 sixth-grade class to a Malcolm X Memorial Service. Later, three prominent Jewish organizations charged him with "black Nazism" because of an article he wrote in the November–December 1967 edition of the *African-American Teachers Forum*, a small mimeographed newsletter. The article, entitled "The

Phenomenon of the Anti-Black Jews and the Black Anglo-Saxons: A Study in Educational Perfidy," suggested that Negro pupils were being "mentally poisoned" by "Jews who dominate the educational bureaucracy of the New York public school system."

The NYU administration apparently had been oblivious to Hatchett's past record. When he took over on July 1, he quietly set about developing his role as a black ombudsman. But on July 23 a routine NYU news release announcing his appointment landed in the hands of Leonard Buder of the *New York Times*. Tipped off by an editor who had asked, "Is this THE John Hatchett?" Buder was on the phone to NYU. He asked if the school was aware of his past. It wasn't. Buder set the record straight in the next morning's paper with a story playing up Hatchett's allegedly anti-semitic article and militant background. Buder later told his friend, NYU administrator Lester Brookner, that the appointment had been a mistake. Why hadn't NYU checked with the New York Board of Education, where they would have found out about his past.

The sensitive New York Jewish community was caught up in the explosive community control controversy in the experimental Ocean Hill-Brownsville school district. Not surprisingly, three Jewish organizations called for Hatchett's dismissal on the day of Buder's article, while across the country the Jewish press called for ouster of the "black Nazi."

As the furor mounted, President Hester, who had been in Germany at the time of Hatchett's hiring, rushed home. His grand urban strategy was boomeranging. Hatchett told the President, "Firing me will turn the entire black community of New York against NYU at the very time you are trying to strengthen your relations to it." The heads of fifteen of NYU's

sixteen student organizations fell in with those who wanted
Hatchett retained. On the other hand, keeping Hatchett
would clearly antagonize NYU's substantial Jewish alumni,
many of whom had contributed to the new black scholarship
fund. Several donors were now threatening to delete NYU
from their wills unless Hatchett was fired. To avoid disaster,
President Hester came up with a grand public-relations answer to this Black-Jew-NYU triangle. He called in two outside mediators who represented the entire spectrum of the
controversy. In former Supreme Court Justice and U.N. Am-
bassador Arthur Goldberg, he had Jewish New York's ranking legal authority. In Federal Judge Constance Baker
Motley, he had a Negro who was the former Borough President of Manhattan and an alumnus and trustee of NYU.
Hatcher met with the two lay leaders and explained that he
was not antisemitic (his family physician, dentist, and lawyer
were all Jewish) and that the "thrust of the article was not
aimed at Jews just because they were Jews. Rather it was anti-
establishment in a school system where 80 to 90 percent of
the teachers and administrators are Jewish."

The mediators recommended that Hatchett be properly
chastized and then retained under a new Afro-American Center board of directors chaired by Judge Motley. In a letter to
President Hester outlining this solution, Goldberg summarily
dismissed Hatchett's viewpoint: "The problems of the New
York City school system and the controversy over decentralization have no relationship whatsoever to any Jewish issue
or personnel." Hester was delighted with this solution—a
rebuke coupled with a stay of execution for Hatchett—and
sought the latter's permission to release the correspondence
to the press. Hatchett was willing to accept the new board of
directors, but he told Hester he would not let Goldberg's

analysis go unchallenged. There followed another meeting in Goldberg's Madison Avenue law office, attended by Hester and Chancellor Allen Cartter, Hatchett, his Jewish lawyer, and several black student leaders. Goldberg, however, was conspicuously absent from the negotiations. The veteran labor mediator told the conferees his solution outlined in the letter was "non-negotiable" and refused to join the meeting. "Goldberg kept walking past the conference room on other business, but he wouldn't come in," recalls Hatchett. Eventually a compromise was hammered out that left Hatchett the right to criticize Goldberg's letter. NYU promptly sent a copy of the letter to all 160,000 alumni.

NYU's decision to retain Hatchett was widely blasted by leading Jewish organizations. In Kansas City the *Jewish Chronicle* editorialized, "We Jews are not a vindictive people . . . but simple dignity demands that he who spits in our face shall not be rewarded." The *New York Post* called the retention of Hatchett "an affront to the memory of Dr. King." In an editorial titled "Mashgiach Goldberg," the Washington, D.C. *Jewish Week* said Goldberg "should not permit himself to issue Kashruth (Kosher) labels to dubious claimants."

But NYU stuck to its decision and gave Hatchett a cautious yellow light to move ahead on his plans. Hatchett's boss, Assistant Chancellor for Student Affairs Harold Whiteman, explained, "He was on a form of probation. I told him 'John, let's get this show on the road. Help us out of this. Stay out of trouble, take it easy.'" During late August and September Hatchett fell out of the limelight and went to work on his administrative program. But resentment smouldered. Hatchett found his promised $150,000 budget cut to $78,000. Established university administrators found the black newcomer brash. Whiteman said, "He looked like he was trying to build an empire. He would storm into a college office and ask for all the records on black students. When he couldn't get them he would accuse the office of concealment. If he wanted this kind of power he should have asked us to make him dean of students." But Hatchett countered that before hiring him NYU had reduced his title twice—from "Dean of Black Student Affairs to Director of Black Student Affairs to Director of the Martin Luther King Center."

In late September, 1968, the administration proudly watched their summer's hard work come to fruition as 500 new Martin Luther King, Jr., scholarship students and 65 Opportunity Award recipients enrolled. But they kept a nervous eye on Hatchett. Said Assistant Chancellor Whiteman, "John still wouldn't get on the administrative team. He still wouldn't take direction." At a freshman orientation meeting Hatchett joked about his administrative responsibility when a student asked if he was antisemitic. "Even though I'm entitled to First Amendment privileges, I'm under a modified form of censorship. I can only work in terms of black and white, so therefore I can't answer the question." He went on to explain, apologetically, that controversy had slowed the center's progress. He said he was working "day and night" because "I'm not an administrator, I'm a teacher. I'm the poorest-assed administrator around here." There was growing agreement on this point at the NYU headquarters in Vanderbilt Hall. Assistant Chancellor Whiteman began to regularly attend Hatchett's speeches along with newspaper reporters watching for hot copy.

Hatchett's militancy even surprised some of the black students. He told them, "I've seen too many natural hairdos housing processed minds. Before [black students] can engage in a real dialogue, we must first understand ourselves." In fact, Hatchett was more action oriented than some of the black student leaders, such as twenty-nine-year-old Winston Duckett, Chairman of the Black Allied Student Association. Duckett, an accounting student, typified NYU blacks who saw the university as a breeding ground for future revolutionaries. He felt, however, that blacks should stick closer to their studies than to the streets while in college, so that they could develop the expertise necessary for the revolution. As he put it, "The University is a tool in my revolution, helping people to power. But you can't fight the revolution like the old days where you line up with muskets and fire. First you've got to get the necessary skills to lead the revolution. After you've learned what you need to know then you can go out and start organizing." Hatchett disagreed. "Some students talked about postponing the revolution until they gain expertise, but I told them 'you have to take the seeds to the black community now, otherwise the black community will reject you; they won't know who you are. You could even do token things like babysitting and cleaning for black parents so they would be free to go to school meetings and get involved in the community."

Hatchett's attempt to lead the black students inevitably triggered his downfall. Good administrators are supposed to be leaders, and John Hatchett tried leading the blacks into action. But in college the savvy administrator knows it is safer to get on the students' backs and slow them down. Recognizing this conflict, Hatchett chose to praise the NYU officials in an October 6, 1968, speech at NYU's University Heights center in the Bronx. He complimented their "intestinal fortitude— even if it's just for this year . . . to stick with me. In the face of massive pressure, they have chosen to recognize the integrity of my intellect, and my right to work with and be responsible to and for black students." Hatchett went on in the same speech to tell the audience that "Nixon, Humphrey and [Teachers Union President Albert] Shanker . . . all have something in common. They are racist bastards." The audience screamed and applauded.

It was a favorite rhetorical technique. He explained later, "The philosophy of my speeches is that there is a great deal of value in shock therapy. If I had just said Humphrey, Nixon and Shanker are racists no one would have raised an eyebrow. But as soon as I used a term considered in bad taste people immediately fastened on it. I didn't mean bastard as a curse or a reference to parentage. I was really just trying to show how liberal Humphrey, conservative Nixon and Shanker—who I just threw in because he was local and relevant—had each bastardized the standards of the country and made the real demands of black people illegitimate."

Hatchett's shock therapy came to breakfasters across the city the following morning on the front page of the *New York Times*. President Hester, who had just arrived in Denver for a conference, immediately flew back to New York, listened to a tape of the speech, and conferred with colleagues all day Wednesday, October 9. Within twenty-four hours Hatchett was fired, and the university senate, composed of twenty-four faculty and twenty-four administrators, had endorsed the action. As Hester said later, "Once we knew we had to do it, we figured we should go ahead and do it quickly, otherwise it would have appeared that we would have been responding to public pressure instead of doing what was right."

The next day, student militants staged a protest strike. Schisms within the black leadership, the inability of black and white leadership to coalesce, and the generally docile attitude of the commuter students rendered the protest ineffective. Uncertain about Hatchett's alleged antisemitism, some Jewish students also withheld support. A few moderate blacks even went to Hatchett and asked him to voluntarily appeal for an end to the protest. Hatchett sighed, "They were worried that they might lose their scholarships if there was a big strike." A hundred students, led by the black militant Katara group, seized two buildings on the University Heights campus in the Bronx. But they withdrew after representatives of the black student group came out of a meeting with President Hester claiming that Hatchett had been reinstated. In fact, Hester had only agreed to let Hatchett become Dean of Black Student Affairs, a post completely independent of the NYU administration. When the militants found out Hatchett was not being rehired, they claimed they had been duped and tried to rebuild protest momentum. But it was too late.

After classes resumed, a fire was set in the student center. It received scant attention in the press, now busily acclaiming Hestor for quelling the incipient revolt. Subsequently, when students offered Hatchett the job of director of an independent Afro-American center, he refused: "Unless I have an official position at NYU, there's no way I can change this racist institution."

To be sure, a few liberal law school faculty complained that the firing of Hatchett violated due process. But President Hester explained that due process was not at issue. "Formal hearing procedures have not been the practice in higher educational institutions for administrative actions of this character. Such actions lie with the president, who must act in the interest of the entire university community."

Thereafter, Hester was very careful to spell out the revised nature of NYU's relationship to the urban community. "New York University can't endorse a particular approach to black power. We don't question Hatchett's right to free speech. It's just that this university is not an agency to develop black consciousness. An official of this university must recognize our diverse responsibilities. This school is a big social institution that exists because society takes us seriously, respects us and wants to support us. Any university president who kept a John Hatchett would alienate his constituency. Even if Hatchett's particular approach would solve the nation's racial problem I couldn't risk NYU's future on him. I don't think you could find a university in this country that could have John Hatchett as an administrator."

With Hatchett out of the way, NYU was able to speed up its urban development plans. To expedite the work, a $222,-500,000 fund drive was planned over the winter. In the spring of 1969, President Hester announced that NYU would invest millions to improve life for all New Yorkers. In addition to three new campus centers for urban studies, NYU faculty would be able to work from endowed urban chairs to solve the problems of the city. Among the fields of specialization would be "mental and physical health of people living in an urban environment, including legal, educational, administrative, financial, and welfare concerns of cities."

After seven years of hard work, President Hester's plans were becoming a reality. "We are experiencing growing interaction of the city and the university, and forecasting a close collaboration in which each can draw upon the strengths of each other. The manifold resources of the university . . . must be enlisted to achieve more effective approaches to the needs of urban society. As we meet these challenges, NYU and other universities must maintain high standards of performance and the academic freedom and institutional autonomy which enables them to perform their most constructive functions in advancing civilization."

# CHAPTER 6

# THE SUBURBAN UNIVERSITY

The northern edge of La Jolla is still one of the few unsubdivided areas between Los Angeles and Tijuana. Here, Torrey Pines State Park preserves the tranquillity of trees blowing in gentle breezes, sculptured cliffs, and unspoiled ocean beaches. Convinced it was an ideal setting for academic repose, the University of California built its San Diego campus there in 1959, on the location of a surplus U.S. Marine Corps base.

Today, 3,700 students study at UCSD. The majority of students are enrolled at Revelle College, an imposing collection of classroom buildings, offices, and dormitories that surrounds a central fountain frequently adorned with practicing flutists.

Up on the third level of the humanities library building at Revelle stands a row of vaultlike offices sharing a common balcony. This is the home of the UCSD Philosophy Department. It is also the office of the most controversial figure in California academic circles today, Professor Herbert Marcuse.

Now ensconced at UCSD, Marcuse works quietly among "old friends." The fact that some of these friends have names like Hegel, Marx, and Lenin has made Professor Marcuse the target of the political right for several years. The fact that he is unwilling to play a more aggressive role, as revolutionary Pied Piper, to today's crop of student activists is now beginning to draw criticism from the left.

After opening the fifteen-foot-high door and going into his office, it wasn't difficult to separate Marcuse's hoary head from those of his companions; their presence was spiritual rather than physical. Marcuse was wearing a rumpled gray sweater, a pair of sunglasses, and a look of undisguised pique accentuated by his furious puffing on a cigarillo. He was rocking back and forth in his chair.

"Look at this!" he said, grabbing a magazine story from his desk. "It's the exact pattern of the Stalinist purge, mixing facts with lies so it is impossible to separate them." The famed Marxist philosopher and author was still fighting off right-wing attacks from the conservative community of San Diego, and one simply assumed this was another American Legion or Birch Society tirade. (The Legion had once offered to pay Marcuse's $20,000 salary for the coming year if he would just quietly leave San Diego. Marcuse refused.) But Marcuse wasn't worrying about the Legion, the Association of Former Grand Jurors of San Diego County, or his other conservative foes this afternoon.

What had outraged him was the latest issue of *PL* magazine, the house organ of the ultraleftist, Peking-oriented
Progressive Labor Party, which carried a piece titled "Marcuse: Cop-Out or Cop?" It suggested the professor was really
a CIA agent in Marxist clothing and pointed out that "G-Man
Marcuse," a refugee from Nazi Germany, had done American intelligence work in the 1940's (he had worked in the
OSS against the Nazis during World War II). It also intimated
that he was now working secretly for the CIA to subvert
student activism and was spying on visiting German intel-
lectuals, whom he ostensibly hosted for the State Department
in San Diego.

*PL*'s charges weren't the only fire he had been getting from
the Left. The San Diego chapter of SDS had been passing
out leaflets in Marcuse's course on Marx and Engels. One
leaflet read: "Marcuse's hesitancy in placing the theories of
Marx into the context of contemporary socialist practice
prohibits a clear understanding of the material." SDS leader
Paula Cate, of Los Angeles, explained: "He's been toning
down the political content of his lectures to avert right-wing
reaction."

The student radicals are equally incensed over Marcuse's
successful efforts to squelch protest demonstrations on the
San Diego campus, most notably the one held after the regents meeting there in November. Marcuse opposes erecting
revolutionary barricades at UCSD and feels the university
sanctuary must be maintained. But beleaguered SDS leaders,
working to build a radical movement at the school, regard
Marcuse's stand as just another handicap. To SDS member
Byron King of San Diego, "Marcuse is a real liability to the
New Left here."

Administrators at UCSD, on the other hand, consider

Marcuse a stabilizing force. Says Chancellor William McGill, who disregarded right-wing sentiment by reappointing Marcuse for the 1969–70 school year, "This is not a very swinging place for kids in the New Left. Those attracted by Marcuse's reputation are disappointed to find that the level of militancy is relatively low. There's no doubt that Marcuse has been a calming influence, forcing students to think through their grievances before moving on to any rash action."

Unfortunately, the same effect can't always be claimed for Marcuse's critics, such as *Pravda* and the San Diego *Union,* SDS, the Young Americans for Freedom, the American Legion, the Progressive Labor Party, Walter Winchell, and Arthur Schlesinger, Jr.

What seems to lie at the heart of Marcuse's almost magnetic ability to attract criticism is a concept he has borrowed from the German philosopher Hegel, which he calls "the power of negative thinking." Oversimplified and summed up, this concept holds that the most fruitful approach to any matter is a negative one. As Hegel put it, "thinking is essentially the negation of that which is immediately before us."

Marcuse explains it this way, "Negative thinking is the term I use for a mode of thinking which does not simply accept the given facts and conditions, but views them in the light of the real possibilities for human freedom which the given facts and conditions often suppress. Negative thought is thus essentially *critical* thought. It is a decisive force in human progress."

It is also a decisive factor in motivating Marcuse's critics, many of whom regard negativism, especially when applied to sacred American institutions, as downright subversive. What they often ignore is Marcuse's contempt for institutions of the left. When Marcuse calls capitalism and communism a pair of sorry bedfellows threatening mankind with their technological and social manipulation, or when he says that "unfreedom is the condition of freedom and war the guarantor of peace," he manages to rock several different boats at one time.

His books probe a variety of social, political and philosophical questions. But whether he is dissecting contemporary society in *One Dimensional Man,* tying up Freud and Marx in *Eros and Civilization,* suggesting that American democracy is really totalitarian in *Critique of Pure Tolerance,* or explaining the failure of Russian Communism in *Soviet Marxism,* his writing remains surprisingly free of preconceptions and political alliances.

Indeed, Marcuse revels in provoking the right and the left with the same work. He points out that *Soviet Marxism* was derided by Soviet critics as an attempt "to deprecate and distort Communist morality," while American critics panned it for treating "Soviet Marxism as a stage in mankind's struggle toward freedom and socialism." Marcuse gleefully takes these apparent contradictions as proof: "I have achieved success in freeing myself from Cold War propaganda."

This iconoclasm also helps explain Marcuse's popularity with some elements of the New Left. In an age where many young people see contemporary political systems as hopelessly obsolete, it is no surprise that they turn to an ideologue who shares their contempt for both modern capitalist and communist societies.

Marcuse is delighted by the young radicals' response. He sees their rebellion as the major hope for the future. "There is an international student apparatus—though it is clearly unorganized—that is reacting to the same kinds of pressures in capitalist and communist countries world-wide," he says. "This growing student revulsion to modern industrial society is my major inspiration today."

Educated at the universities of Berlin and Freiburg, he was a member of the Sparticist movement, a revolutionary social-ist group active in Germany after World War I. After he fled the Nazi regime and came to America, he turned to radical scholarship. Marcuse guest lectured at Harvard and Colum-bia, but he didn't turn exclusively to teaching until he went to Brandeis University in 1954 (after working for Institutes at Columbia and Harvard and serving the Office of Strategic Services during the 40's). Marcuse stayed at Brandeis until his retirement in 1965. During that period he took time out for guest lectureships at the University of Paris in 1958 and 1960-61.

"Students at San Diego are as bright a group as I've ever seen," says Marcuse. "They are serious, diligent, enthusias-tic." But while young radicals flock to his classroom—as well as his lectures in New York, Berlin and Paris—he will not map out a revolutionary program for them.

"To develop a revolutionary program," he says, "one has to be able to actively implement it. That's impossible for me, so I could not even consider trying to push the youth in a specific direction. Besides, that would be foolish. If the young develop a revolutionary program, it will be a unique product of their own experience. Their mistrust for the 'central com-mittee' approach suggests they understand the liability of too much planning. At this point I believe revolution in America is a mistake—taking to the barricades is far too dangerous. Now it is far better to work within the universities, in small groups, inside the structure. Abroad I have had little impact on the students." As for the charge that he was a moving force in last year's Paris student uprising, Marcuse says, "The French translation of *One Dimensional Man* was not even on the newsstands until after the May rebellion began."

While Marcuse may not be a revolutionary, San Diego in general and La Jolla in particular scarcely seem the ideal places for a Marxist philosopher to crown his career. California's higher education system is blessed by state munificence but plagued by political intolerance. As late as the 1950s, vigilantes like American Legion leader Harry Foster had San Diego State psychology professor Harry Steinmetz successfully purged for his refusal to answer questions on Communist affiliations. There were similar firings at Berkeley, and Stanford alumni pressured for the ouster of the late Marxist economist Paul Baran in the early sixties.

Furthermore, San Diego is a bulwark of the military-industrial establishment, which is so alien to Marcuse. It is home base for $12,000,000,000 worth of military ships and planes. The military payroll is $432,000,000 annually, and local defense concerns produce over $640,000,000 worth of aircraft and missile products each year.

Much of the state's wealth is in La Jolla, a relaxed, upper-middle-class community where executives and retirees can count their change in peace and quiet. The main street faithfully shuts down at 6 P.M. every day. Only the Merrill Lynch office remains open for nocturnal stock investment classes. It seems incongruous that Marcuse, who has been so hard on the affluent ("People recognize themselves in their commodities; they find their soul in their automobile, hi-fi set, split-level home, kitchen equipment."), would want to move in with them.

Until ten years ago Marcuse, who is Jewish, would not have been able to find a home in La Jolla. To keep out minority buyers, local realtors exchanged green slips on prospects. Real estate man Joseph Becker explains it this way: "If the realtor felt a prospective buyer was undesirable he put 'positive' on the slip. If he was desirable he wrote 'negative.' This slip was passed among realtors. It was a terrible system and I refused to participate." Finally, under pressure from local university officials, who were hiring numerous Jewish professors, the covenant was dropped.

Marcuse says that climate and locale outweighed all other factors in his move to San Diego, after retiring from Brandeis in 1965. "At my age the climate is ideal and, as you know, this is one of the few unspoiled areas left in Southern California. Of course I knew there might be political problems, but I really didn't worry about it." UCSD was delighted to get Marcuse. Explains Chancellor McGill, "This campus started off in 1958 as a science school, an outgrowth of the Scripps Institute of Oceanography. We wanted to develop first-rate humanities departments. One of the best ways is to bring in distinguished older men like Marcuse, who attract hot young professors."

So Marcuse settled down in a pleasant suburban home within walking distance of the campus. With him were his wife, a flock of loyal graduate students who followed him from Brandeis, and his old battered Peugeot. (Thickening his German accent, Marcuse says, "I could never think of buying an American car. Total waste.") His arrival was noted routinely in the local press, and there was no trouble for the first two years, since most rightist sentiment was aimed at a colleague, Dr. Richard Popkin, who once told a local audience that "law and order can be carried too far."

But then in July, 1967, Marcuse told an appreciative student audience in Berlin, "We have to develop *the political implications* of the moral, intellectual and sexual rebellion of the youth." The San Diego *Union* called this "bad taste," asked the United States to apologize to the West German government, and suggested that the UC regents investigate Marcuse. In May 1968, Marcuse spoke again in Germany and in France. He conferred with North Vietnamese peace representatives in Paris and met with Berlin student leader Rudi Dutschke, then recovering from an attempted assassination. When a national magazine erroneously reported that Marcuse had invited Dutschke to study at UCSD, local papers immediately demanded an investigation. The American Legion joined other rightist groups in calling for Marcuse's dismissal. Representative Bob Wilson, a Republican from San Diego, demanded that the State Department deny Dutschke's visa application.

The furor prompted a spate of abusive mail, including a death threat that read, "Marcuse, you are a very dirty Communist dog. We give you seventy-two hours to live [*sic*] United States. Seventy-two hours more, Marcuse, and we kill you—Ku Klux Klan." After his phone was cut off the next day by an anonymous order, Marcuse and his wife left town for two weeks of seclusion in Carmel.

To this day he insists it was a phantom issue. "Rudi is one of the most brilliant students I have ever known. When I met him in Berlin, he told me he planned to visit Boston to consult neurosurgeons for his head wounds. I suggested that he might come to San Diego to visit, but there was never anything about his becoming a student."

In the end, Dutschke canceled his trip and withdrew his visa application. This made little difference to Marcuse's enemies. When school opened in the fall of 1968, they renewed their cries for his ouster.

Working out of his suite in the U.S. Grant Hotel, sixty-nine-year-old American Legion leader Harry L. Foster was a prime mover in the campaign against Marcuse. He was aided by the San Diego *Union,* which ran editorials urging Marcuse's ouster with headlines such as "This Is An Order." Legion Post 6 raised $20,000 overnight in an attempt to buy Marcuse's contract from UCSD. Post 6 Commander George Fischer said the university could become a "foundation for some of the world's outstanding radicals" if Marcuse stayed. He added, "I think it is worth it to the community and the university to get rid of him."

As a matter of fact, overage appointments like Marcuse's had to be approved by the UC Board of Regents, a group scarcely sympathetic to Marxist philosophers. But some clever politicking in 1968 put Marcuse's fate in the hands of UCSD's new chancellor, William McGill. The way it came about was this:

In the summer of 1967 the UCSD Physics department was trying to hire Dr. Linus Pauling, the only two-time Nobel laureate other than Madame Curie. Because he was then sixty-six, Pauling's appointment had to be decided on by the regents, and UCSD officials were worried because Pauling's antiwar activities might prompt the regents to reject him. So, at the urging of San Diego officials, President Charles Hitch of UC persuaded the regents to delegate authority on all overage appointments to each individual campus. The maneuver was handled so delicately that the regents voted over their authority on May 17, 1968, completely unaware of Pauling's pending appointment. Chancellor McGill recalls, "I just had to laugh that day as I watched Reagan and [Lieutenant Governor Robert] Finch and all those other conservative regents voting for Linus Pauling."

Of course Pauling was miffed by the delay. "The department said I could start in the fall of 1967. But then the administration decided to get the rules changed before giving
me an appointment. That took them nine months and then
they didn't even send me my notice of appointment until July
10, 1968—ten days after it was effective."

Chancellor McGill handled Marcuse's reappointment with
the same infinite delicacy. First, he got the American Legion
to quiet down so he could study the matter "free from pressure." The reappointment matter was then channeled
through a half-dozen campus committees. Says McGill, "Obviously we couldn't make any decision until after the 1968
presidential election. I told the philosophy department I
didn't want to see any information on Marcuse until October.
They reported in December." The reappointment was finally
made by McGill in mid-February. The conservative UC regents were upset by the decision and took back their control
on overage appointments in April of 1969. This makes Marcuse's reappointment next year look doubtful. Pauling has
already left UCSD for Stanford, citing the "uncertainty" of
political factors on the Board of Regents as the cause.

Chancellor McGill says that "Professor Marcuse has indicated he wants to retire. If he decides to change his mind and
seek reappointment, I seriously doubt if we would seek approval from the Regents. I am sure that if we did it would be
denied." Whether Marcuse retires from, or is forced out of,
UCSD, he has many options open. For one thing, he has
standing job offers from several prestigious universities.

There is also the added consolation of book royalties. *One
Dimensional Man* alone has sold over 100,000 copies in
sixteen languages. His works are best-sellers at La Jolla book-
stores, boosted, no doubt, by the front-page space in papers

like the *Union,* and there are numerous speaking offers from around the world.

Should Marcuse be pushed out of San Diego in 1970, he will leave a major gap in the campus faculty. At seventy, he is at the pinnacle of his academic prominence, and despite SDS criticism, he remains the most popular professor on campus. The philosopher generates a healthy academic turmoil in the classroom. Says Erica Sherover, a doctoral candidate who doubles as Marcuse's research assistant, "He's at his best when dealing with leftists who've swallowed a lot of jargon. They expound theories and he says 'What do you mean by that?' He forces them to expose their ignorance."

In class Marcuse comes on like the teutonic master. About to convene a "Marx and Lenin" lecture, he silences gossiping students by coming up behind them and poking them gently with his pointer. He begins class by promoting an extracurricular discussion of the SDS leaflet that has attacked his teaching methods. He asks "Could we meet next Monday night?"

Student heads nod, but one boy laments, "That's the night of the jazz concert."

"Very well," says Marcuse. "We shall put the two together."

After the laughter subsides, Marcuse lectures on Marxian theory. "Moral judgments do not play any role in capitalism. The theory calls for a specific social and political practice. There's not the slightest indication in Marx of capitalist conspiracy or conspiracy of the upper class. There is no theory of the evil character of capitalists. Even if all capitalists are angels, there would still be disintegration and a need for radical change."

After one class, SDS leader Paula Cate said she was disappointed by Marcuse's refusal to illustrate Marx with examples from today's China and Cuba. "For example," she said, "when someone asked him who would do the work no one likes to do under utopian socialism, Marcuse humorously suggested Fourier's theories on the four-year-olds, who naturally like to collect garbage." But, Paula explained, Marcuse had a number of current examples close at hand. She cited the Cuban students who help harvest sugar and the Chinese philosophy professor who drives a tractor and is the leader of his commune.

Her complaint is echoed by many who have read Marcuse. Readers of varying political viewpoints see him obsessed with criticisms of present-day society, without offering any alternatives. The student radicals complain that he refuses to back their free university proposals, or support their efforts to ally the San Diego working class with the student movement. He had, in short, given the New Left little or no plan of action to complement his classroom ideology.

Why?

To begin with, Marcuse feels that scholarship is the background of any revolutionary movement. He likes to remind radicals that Lenin read Hegel three times before he moved into action. "You must read first, you need a theoretical understanding before you can hope to change things."

Marcuse also believes that, as an academic, he has no right to become actively involved in anyone else's revolution. At the end of his essay on "Repressive Tolerance," he dismisses his own writing as "abstract and academic." He is determined not to become the elder statesman of the student movement, the New Left, or "the revolution." He said he has turned down speaking offers in Cuba three times. "I don't know Spanish and I don't like to use a translator."

Marcuse also doubts he will make much difference to the future. He is not performing surgery, but only making a diagnosis. His major source of inspiration, he says, is the inevitability of change. "Changing the system may take ten, twenty or fifty years—maybe even longer. But sooner or later the system will change. Otherwise it will be the first system in history that hasn't."

In the meantime, Marcuse will continue to write and teach. A major measure of his success will be the rancor of his critics. As he explains, "Somehow, somewhere, what I say must really hit and hurt, must drive home some unwelcome truths. Typically, the reaction is not argument from the brain, but foam from the mouth.

"The right accuses me of being an agent of Moscow or Peking. Professor Schlesinger, in the middle, reproaches me for advocating violence and undermining democracy. *Pravda* denounced me for undermining the revolution by reformist and revisionist theories. Whether I am charged with working for the Pentagon or for the Kremlin, for the Nazis or for the Chinese, for or against the students, whether I am accused of having eaten my father or my son, I shall do with these charges what they deserve: Nothing."

# CHAPTER 7:

# THE HIGH SCHOOLS

Calumet High School is black but not beautiful. It is a block-long, C-shaped building which retains its old red-brick veneer, and the gargoyles that greeted the Polish kids who used to go there on their way up the social ladder. Today, the all-black enrollment of 3,000 is twice the building's capacity, and the interior no longer looks like a way station for the upwardly mobile. The checkerboard floors are scuffed beyond the help of any wax, toilets have no tissue, sinks are without soap. A filthy teachers' washroom doubles as a book storeroom. Weeks pass before a light bulb is replaced, a blackboard washed off, or a clock fixed. Walls and bulletin boards often have two coats of graffitti, with slogans like

"Panther Power Now," scrawled over the old crudities like "JM sucks cock."

Given this environment, it is not surprising that the 58-year-old white principal Charles LaForce is a beleaguered man. A former shop teacher and a veteran of thirty years in the Chicago school system, he has discovered that black student power is not just an external phenomenon imported only on the anniversaries of the assassinations of Malcolm X and Martin Luther King. True, February and April traditionally bring disruptions in the lunchroom and fires in the lavatory wastebaskets. But in the fall of 1968, the school was in continuous turmoil. Hundreds of students participated in a city-wide boycott during September and October. There were sporadic incidents during November, building up to a fortnight of chaos just before Christmas.

The crisis at Calumet is mirrored in public school systems across the country. One educational survey taken during the 1968–69 year shows that "three out of five principals report some form of active protest in their schools," while most of the rest "expect it in the near future." From November to February, 239 "serious episodes"—strikes, sit-ins, demonstrations or riots—occurred in American high schools. Big city school systems like Pittsburgh, Miami, New York and Detroit were in constant turmoil. While most of the protests centered around race and the Vietnam war, many others were directed against archaic dress regulations and tight academic strictures. By the end of the 1960's there is more trouble in American secondary schools than in American colleges. Indeed, the high schools are beginning to look more and more like the minor leagues for student dissidents who will soon move up to the major league battlegrounds in the colleges.

Of course, high school educators disagree on the reasons for the trouble. Chicago Board of Education member Thomas Murray blames "the introduction of sex education into the curriculum." W. R. Robbins, principal of an Austin, Texas, high school blames parents. "When students begin to demand something, I think it shows poor breeding." At suburban Buffalo's Amherst Central High School where students still pledge allegiance to the flag each morning, attendance supervisor Alan Schaefer feels, "It's all filtered down from the college. These high school radicals don't have an original idea. If the junior high kids could start growing beards they would. If the girls could they would too."

But none of these theories help explain what is happening at Calumet and other high schools across the country. Chained to a vision of the past, secondary educators try to make high schools into the first line of defense against social change.

Take Madison's West High School, near the University of Wisconsin. Students there have been suspended for wearing mustaches (which "distract" others) and NAACP sweatshirts ("commercialism"). A police photographer, dressed college-style, is occasionally planted at the high school's side door to look for narcotics users. He uses the school yearbook as a wanted poster.

At all-black Anderson High School in Austin, Texas, football-coach-turned-principal, W. E. Pigford, keeps hair short and skirts long. He yearns for the good old days when "Every boy on the team and I went to church the Sunday before a big game—and to the same church too. Today, nobody cares about church anymore. We've got three parking lots and we still can't take care of all the cars."

Sincere administrators are often victimized by communities that try to pour all their obsolete values into the high schools. Fourteen years after *Brown vs. Board of Education* outlawed school segregation, Tuscaloosa, Alabama, Senior High School is only 7 percent black. But even the fledgling "black power" activities of this minority are too much for this town of 63,000. During a pep rally in the fall of 1968, black students responded to the waving of confederate flags by raising their fists in a "Black Power" chant. Principal Hugh Stegall quickly called both black and white leaders together and worked out a compromise. The blacks were prohibited from waving their fists and the whites from waving their flags. He also agreed to reduce the number of renditions of "Dixie" at each pep rally, but pointed out, "It will be a while before we can abolish 'Dixie' altogether. The whites of this community are conservative."

Often the high school teachers are more of a roadblock than the community. In Washington, D.C., a new, ambitious black principal at Eastern High School has helped set up a fully accredited, student-run freedom school in a nearby church. With administrative aid, the students raised $85,000, recruited teachers, and established curriculums. About eighty-five students take regular morning classes at Eastern and then are bused to the freedom school annex in the afternoon. There they study black history, literature, economics, and Swahili. Classes begin and end to the tune of a James Brown record.

But back at Eastern High School proper, the freedom school annex is regarded with suspicion by veteran white teachers. They criticized Principal William J. Saunders once for joining the students in an "I'm black and I'm proud" chant during an assembly. While the *Washington Post* and *Time* gave the school extensive coverage, the veteran advisor of the high school paper refused to run a feature on the subject. Instead, she inserted articles like "Students, Catch On" which pointed out, "Reports are coming in that companies are taking a long cold look at graduates who come from protesting colleges."

It would, of course, be a mistake to try to find a typical American high school. On the other hand, a number of schools like Chicago's Calumet do provide a sketch of the factors causing the high school upsurge. Although Principal LaForce is scarcely representative, like many of his colleagues across the country he desperately clings to his authority and vision of the past. The teachers, for their part, fear students who no longer revere them.

Still, Calumet is not the worst of what Chicago has to offer. Located between 81st and 82nd streets, well beyond the core poverty belt, it is in a modest, but not impoverished, district. Surveys show that over half the students enter with IQ's above 90, and that the average freshman arrives with a sixth-grade reading level. In the next four years his reading level will progress two years—slightly better than the average Chicago ghetto high school student. Over 40 percent of the Calumet graduates go on to some form of higher education.

The students come each fall with high hopes. But from the moment they walk through the heavy doors there is confusion and discouragement. Sometimes it takes half a semester to get their class-election cards straightened out. They can't move from basic to advanced course tracks because their home room teachers don't know how to program changes on the IBM sheets. Tardy or absent students often wait until noon before they are processed through the long attendance office line.

When students finally get into the right classes, they find their problems continue to abound. Under school board procedures, textbook allotments are not made until after a fall headcount. By the time the textbooks are ordered and received, fifteen or twenty classes will still be entirely without texts, and many others shorthanded. The teachers, many of them substitutes, offer uneven curriculums. Gwendolyn Cherry, a timid honors student who works as a part-time clerk in the principal's office, complains, "Our classes never get anywhere. In history, whether you take Early or Contemporary World, or Modern World, or World Geography, it's always the same. The teacher begins with Christopher Columbus and ends with the First World War. We always take time for Dred Scott, but I'm still waiting to find out about Russia and Germany." A few exceptional students are allowed to take courses at a nearby city college. Most of the "basic" or "remedial" students are dumped into large, unwieldy classes, where the teacher spends half the period taking the roll and keeping order.

While the Board of Education may be color blind in assigning principals and teachers, the students still sense racial innuendoes. For example, senior class president Joe Griffin explains, "When a white teacher says 'I'm with you people all the way,' that's his first mistake. I'd much rather have him get up and say 'I'm a racist' than have him pretend to be the great white father bringing light to all us little darkies."

Another source of irritation are the ID cards all Calumet students must carry. Theoretically, these are used for code numbers on course sheets, but the administration makes wider use of them. Not only does a student have a number and a picture, but his entire schedule is filled in on the card. He may be asked to show his ID in the corridor, lunchroom, attendance office, or the bathroom. As one irate boy puts it, "Can you imagine a white school where the principal walks around asking students to produce their mug shots? I guess his problem is that all of us look alike." The students also dislike exchange programs that bring white students to look at their school. Says a sophomore girl, "People come visiting here like it was a monkey house. Everyone knows what this place is like, but when others come it's worse."

Not surprisingly, a good number of bright students, especially boys, turn off early. In most classes, the boys sit dejectedly in the back of the room while the teacher conducts class with the girls. One instructor who has tried to reverse the trend is black Roy Stell, who teaches five Afro-American history sections. Stell recognizes that he attracts many of the most hostile students who see the three R's as a honkie invention. To break down the barrier, he will walk to the back of the class, tap a dozing student on the shoulder and say, "Thank you very much for coming today; now go back to sleep." In discussion, he lets the students make value judgments on a book they haven't read—to encourage them to read it. For example, one day he introduced the Kerner report with the innocuous question, "Who wrote this book?" A girl piped up, "The man wrote it. Why is it that white people never believe black people unless it's verified by other white people?" As Stell notes after class, "You have to flush out the poison, make them rip it apart before most of these students will even want to look at a white man's book." A few days later, the chapter-by-chapter oral reports began and almost everybody participated. Still, in most classes, even the best students show very little enthusiasm. Lonnie Gray, a fifteen-year-old sophomore and honors student says wistfully, "When I think about coming to this place in the morning, I just want to turn over and go back to sleep. I wish school could be like those science fiction movies where you learn from a television right by your bed."

Tension builds quickly in this environment. During the fall of 1968, after a city-wide boycott brought 30,000 pupils out of class on four successive Mondays, the Calumet African Student Organization (CASO) began circulating a list of twenty-eight demands. Included were demands for a black studies department, a student-faculty review board, and rejuvenation of the Calumet plant. Principal LaForce chose to ignore the grievances for several months, engaging in the Alphonse-and-Gaston act with School Superintendent James Redmond. While Redmond was telling dissatisfied parents and citizens to work out their problems at the local level, LaForce was claiming that the demands would have to be met at the school board level.

Thus the inevitable spiral began. First the principal angered large numbers of students by denying the Homecoming Queen, who was a CASO member, the traditional bouquet of flowers. Then he tried to brush aside student "negotiators" as unrepresentative. So the students formed an umbrella organization called the Black Student Advisory Council and demanded a "yes" or "no" answer to each of their demands. LaForce tried to explain the demands away, but the students were tired of listening. "I barely had the qualifications out of my mouth," recalls the principal, "when they got up and walked out." In early December, in a fit of anger, he made the fatal mistake of trying to suspend one of the militant leaders. The result was violence.

Several students smashed the rickety, nail-ridden furniture outside the principal's office. A few days later, the leaders provoked a demonstration aimed at stirring up the entire

student body. As one CASO member explained, "A fight
was faked at the back of the lunchroom and then people
started throwing plates and food from the front to create
mass panic. Cherry bombs were set off in the halls, fires lit in
the bathrooms, and Protect-U (a mace-like repellant ob-
tained from auto supply warehouses) sprayed around the
floors. "We were very careful not to endanger lives. As a
matter of fact, only one person was hurt during the entire
demonstration when she fell down some stairs. You can get
hurt like that any day just by being trampled in the halls."
Before noon, school was dismissed for the weekend.

The following Monday, LaForce agreed to discuss the
demands at a series of assemblies, but again the leaders felt
he was trying to "psych" them out with threats rather than
concessions. They led a walk-out after several assemblies
and proceeded to break some furniture. Eventually the principal called in parents to patrol the halls. They restored
calm. Thereafter, he lived in almost constant fear of further
violence.

The tragedy of Calumet and so many black schools under
white leadership, is that their principals fail to understand
that chaos and violence are largely reflections of their own
timidity, fear, and disorganization. Before coming to Calumet in 1964 (when it was still predominantly white), La-
Force spent nine years as an elementary principal in the
tough Lawndale district. Nevertheless, LaForce has never
felt comfortable at Calumet. He rarely sits down, holds conferences with faculty members at their mailboxes, and listens
with a fidgety, far-off look in his eyes. He rejects any artificial
separation from students, preferring to play the role of patrol-
man. When in his office, he keeps the door open and bird-dogs
the slightest noise. In the corridors, he asks students for hall

passes, and rips improperly posted announcements off bulletin boards.

Obviously, LaForce is being victimized, in part, by a social revolution. "The black people are achieving their place in society and feeling their power," he says a bit ruefully. "I was at a cocktail party recently where everybody was giving me advice on how to run the school. Finally, I just said, 'Look, what you think, or I think, doesn't amount to a kettle of beans. When you're in a ghetto school, you're through thinking. If you're white, you're wrong.' "

It is easy to understand why LaForce is so pessimistic. Not only are the students hostile, but he faces an open revolt from faculty members, who are tired of the confusion. For white and black teachers, maintaining order alone is a full-time job. They feel that anarchy exists in the administration as well. For instance, teachers complain that there are no regular staff meetings, no announcements of personnel changes (such as those for new student counselors), and no bulletins or handbooks explaining such basic things as the requirements for graduation. In a faculty of 130 members, with 50 full-time substitutes, the lack of centralized authority is a desperate problem.

At a university, the faculty usually concerns itself with broad matters of policy and leaves the day-to-day details to the chairman. In a black high school, the day-to-day problems are the central concern. For example, when special assemblies are announced without warning (as they frequently are) and shoved into the morning schedule, the day's timetable is completely upset. The faculty becomes discouraged by the principal's overreliance on his long-time white assistants and unwillingness to delegate authority. In a typical gesture, LaForce appointed, "for the day," an acting black chairman for the math department. This was in September of 1968. Having forgotten about the appointment altogether, he approached the man six months later and asked, "Are you still the chairman?" Afterward the teacher remarked, "If I had any authority, I might be able to do something about the math curriculum. At the present time, there is no curriculum. It's not on paper; it's not in the files; it's not in my head. So we just have a bunch of strung-together courses that have been left over for ten years." As an index of faculty confusion and dissatisfaction, a group of staff members presented LaForce with a list of suggestions in March of 1969. The first suggestion was that he draw up an organizational chart with job descriptions for all administrators, including himself.

The faculty is also beset by racial tension. "Until recently," says a biology instructor, "the teacher's lounge was like a kindergarten class. The whites would play bridge on one side and have their own coffee pot. The blacks would play whist on the other and have their own coffee." At the heart of the racial division is Chicago's anachronistic certification procedure. Unlike most cities which accept transcripts and experience alone, Chicago requires that prospective teachers take both written and oral tests. White oral examiners often reject black teachers who don't adhere to a white dialect. But this discrimination does not bar the teachers from the classroom. Because of the city's teacher shortage, they become full-time basic substitutes holding regular faculty positions. Some FTBS retire after twenty years without ever receiving certification. They are deprived of salary advances beyond the fourth level ($8,000) and certain seniority privileges. As a result, they become bitter second-class citizens venting their hostility on the older, certified whites who regard them as inferior.[1]

During the December crisis, all the faculty tensions congealed in a bitter two-hour meeting which was called after students had rioted and been dismissed early. Many teachers were more concerned about getting home early that day than they were in the problems of Calumet. Nevertheless, there was a sense of desperation in their meeting. The fooball coach, hardly a militant organizer, said a bit sadly, "The students today felt there was nothing inside of Calumet to attract them. There is something lacking here—even the brainy youngsters, good athletes and student leaders don't feel the need to stay. There was no intimidation. The students are speaking with one voice." One white teacher, claiming that the violence had been instigated by "outsiders wearing dew rags," was aghast. The social studies chairman condemned students and sympathetic faculty members for the "beer hall putsch. . . . I reject this authoritarian fascism, black, white, Nazi, whatever it is." Other faculty members suggested that the school be closed down for further dialogue, but neither the principal nor district superintendent had the authority to do it. They asked the handful of student sympathizers, like Roy Stell, to try to meet with the rebels and pacify them.

Stell refused, saying, "I don't think you want to give a 'condescending' inch. What are you trying to run here—a penitentiary or something?" Finally the faculty accepted the principal's suggestion that parents be called in to patrol the halls.

[1]In the May, 1969 teacher contract settlement, the superintendent agreed to phase out oral certification tests. In addition, certification would become automatic for FTBS with 3-years experience and a satisfactory principal's recommendation. The hostilities generated by the old system are not likely to dissolve quickly.

As an outgrowth of the crisis, some positive steps were taken. The parents, understanding the bitterness of their children at first hand, pressed LaForce to meet some of the demands—which he did. For example, he appointed an additional black chairman and black assistant principal, and removed the pictures of George Washington from the halls. Two special before-school classes were set up to give both college-bound and remedial seniors one last-ditch review of all the material they should have learned during four years of school. The math teacher, for example, covered decimals to calculus in five weeks. The teachers began formulating their own demands and integrating the lounges. The students found the administration more attentive by the spring of 1969.

Unfortunately, the calm was destined to be short-lived. As the year came to an end, more than thirty teachers were requesting transfers, or retiring. LaForce himself requested a "lateral transfer." When a group of Calumet parents went to the area superintendent seeking the appointment of a black principal, they were rebuffed. The superintendent was in a rage. "Did you come here to take up my time with this? Your children are doing better than those in other ghetto areas. Why aren't you satisfied?"

# CHAPTER 8

# THE WAR AGAINST THE RADICALS

A seventeen-year-old Midwestern high school senior proved completely candid in his interview with the Oberlin College admissions officer. Heavily involved in the antiwar movement, the student spoke out rabidly against American imperialism. As he droned on the Oberlin official scribbled notes over the young man's folder, "Here's a classic case. A National Liberation Front member. Every cliché at his grasp. Very difficult to pin down." A fast-talking Jewish youth and his dad prompted a similar reaction from another Oberlin counselor. "He and his father remind me of the 'typical Jews' cliché. Pusher, aggressive, talker, high goals."

Five years ago such comments probably would have led

the liberal Oberlin faculty to shake up the school's admissions department. But when student members of the campus admissions committee released these and similar comments, the faculty promptly dismissed them from the committee as indiscreet undergraduates. As Oberlin Admissions official Robert Jenkins explained, "The comments didn't raise faculty fears about possible discrimination. They were much more upset about irreparable damage done to the school's image by this breach of confidentiality."

Attempts to siphon off "pushy, aggressive," future SDS types are the logical extension of a new national movement on college radicals. At a time when the American public is increasingly confused about which foreign countries are allies and which are enemies, almost everyone is in agreement that campus activists are a clear and present danger to the national well being. A recent Harris Poll shows that 90 percent of the country favors a "crackdown on hippie student protest groups." Even morticians are worried about the effects of protest on their recruitment of young talent. An editorial in the *American Funeral Director* warns that a college degree no longer provides automatic assurance that "a young person will serve the public and his employer in a manner that will lend prestige to funeral service. Too many of those attending college are just plain young punks, who have little respect for law and order . . . their country and the rights of others."

Like an angry parent cutting off his son's allowance, the federal government struck back by cancelling financial aid to rebellious students. Campus administrators sent junior to his room—in the county jail—while police administered spankings with nightsticks, mace, dogs, gas, and guns.

The McClellan committee subpoenaed records on campus radicals and their organizations from Berkeley, Stanford,

Harvard, and numerous other schools. Justice department officials suggested that demonstrators "should be rounded up and put in a detention camp." Reports circulated that J. Edgar Hoover had already begun to distribute to his regional offices lists of people who should be picked up for "preventive detention" under the McCarran Act. President Nixon added that further reprisals were in the offing. "We have the power to strike back if need be, and to prevail."

Meanwhile state officials were prodded by their irate constituents into the campus decency parade. In Pennsylvania, House Democratic Leaders sent all campus administrators a list of twenty state laws applicable to student rioters. Among them was the criminal statute against "Blasphemy—derogation or irreverant references to God, Christ, the Holy Spirit or the Scriptures." The punishment was a $100 fine and up to thirty days in jail. In California 200 new bills introduced in the state legislature threatened everything from walling off campuses to abolition of student-initiated courses. When Wisconsin Governor Warren Knowles proposed a bill to expel trouble-makers from campus for one year, the state legislature moved to make it two.

Men willing to lead this fight against the students have found themselves richly rewarded. S. I. Hayakawa's tough stand at San Francisco State vaulted him overnight from a part-time professor to the Gallup Poll's educator of the year. Even on tranquil campuses savvy administrators have made a name for themselves by using threats to attain their goals. Notre Dame president Theodore Hesburgh won national publicity when he announced that sit-inners would be arrested after a fifteen-minute warning. President Nixon rewarded Hesburgh by naming him chairman of the U.S. Civil Rights Commission. Hesburgh replaced Michigan State University President John Hannah, who was taking over the Agency for International Development. In his farewell address at MSU, retiring President Hannah pleaded for faculty endorsement of police action against demonstrators. Afterward Hannah and an audience of 500 sneaked out the back door of a Fairchild Auditorium under a police guard that shielded them from an angry student group protesting the firing of a radical political science professor.

A whole new band of educators like Hannah have joined the crusade against the "New Barbarians." NYU philosopher Sidney Hook has criss-crossed the country to organize moderate faculty and administrators against "anarchists." The media also got into the act. A liberal *New York Times* editorialist suggested, "These disturbed and disturbing youngsters should be expelled. The university is not a residence facility for the psychiatrically maladjusted." The *New Republic* demanded the immediate expulsion of disruptive students and Drew Pearson suggested that protestors at San Francisco State be sentenced to ninety days at cleaning up the Union Oil mess off Santa Barbara beaches. CBS editorialist-in-residence Eric Sevareid prophesized that, "If the young do start a revolution, it will be only symbolistic. But the repression that will move to stop it will be realistic."

Sure enough officials became frustrated by the inability of their new laws to effectively squelch radicals and began to escalate the charges. At Ohio State in Columbus blacks were arraigned on kidnapping charges after they held a vice-president captive in his office for eight hours. In Oakland seven Berkeley leaders of a march against the local draft induction center in October 1967 found themselves in triple jeopardy. First they were suspended by the university, then they were prosecuted for trespassing and finally they were prosecuted for felonious conspiracy to commit a misdemeanor (trespassing). These trumped up charges did not stand up in court. The seven Berkelely conspirators were acquitted and charges against the Columbus kidnappers were dropped.

But officials soon discovered they could drive their points home without actual convictions. Prosecution alone was enough to put some radicals out of action. Take the case of twenty-five-year-old Floyd Nichols of Houston, Texas. The slim junior hardly fits the black bourgeois image portrayed on the catalogue cover of Texas Southern University (enrollment 4,500). It features a Brooks Brothers clad Negro, attaché case in hand, setting off for work at Southwestern Bell Telephone. As a SNCC leader, Nichols helped lead TSU students in a drive against local racism. As he explained it, "I was getting an education but I wasn't doing anything to help the black people outside the school. In Houston, blacks are completely powerless. It's the kind of a town where pregnant ladies are arrested for missing a house payment." So during the 1966–67 school year, Nichols and his SNCC friends organized around a host of on-and off-campus issues. In May of 1967, Nichols was involved in a demonstration at recently integrated Northwood Junior High School where black students had been suspended after defending themselves against white toughs.

On May 17, Nichols and his TSU friends Charles Freeman and Douglas Waller drove twenty miles to Northwood Junior High School for a day of picketing. In the early evening, after police had arrested twenty-eight of the demonstrators, the three drove back to campus where they met fellow students who had been picketing to force the closure of the Sunnyside Dump on the south side of town. This protest had been triggered by the death of a black child who had stumbled into the open dump and perished. Nichols learned that police had arrested 36 demonstrators. About 8:30 p.m. Houston policemen, who had been shadowing campus activists with cameras and tape recorders for months, arrived on campus, recognized Waller and ordered him to leave campus. When he refused he was arrested. Nichols then drove to northeast Houston with Freeman and spent the night protecting a black family from racist cross-burners.

After Nichols and Freeman left TSU the police put thirty vehicles around the periphery of the tense campus. Caged dogs from canine squads barked at students on the way to their rooms. Helmeted riot police stood watch. Ambulances and paddy wagons were carefully deployed. In disgust one student tossed a piece of watermelon at a police car, at which point 500 police reinforcements began taking their positions. Around midnight, Houston Police Chief Herman Short, directing operations from behind a tree, told his men to open up on alleged sniper fire coming from the dorm. He urged caution however. "There are innocent people in there and we don't want them hurt." Irate students tossed bottles while building huge bonfires of tarwood between the police and the dorm. Finally at 1:25 A.M., Chief Short decided to lead a charge against Lanier Hall. "I'm gonna clean that dorm out. I was hoping we wouldn't have to go in there, but we're going to have to stop it before they burn the place down or kill someone."

The cops moved in, pouring thousands of rounds of ammunition into the dormitory. They killed one of their own officers with a ricochet bullet and injured two others. Enraged, they charged into the dormitory, broke open doors with axes and smashed everything in sight. The police stepped on Housemother Mattie Herbert, and demolished her typewriter, television, sewing machine, and coffee urn. Students were dragged out of bed, beaten, herded into the corridor, bitten by snarling dogs, and kicked downstairs. Clad only in their underwear, they were forced to lie prone on grassy campus anthills. The police rounded up a total of 486 students and trucked them off to the Harris County Jail. To their surprise, the students found the jail officials had been expecting them all day. Apparently forewarned of the riot, turnkeys had seen to it that extra mattresses were taken out of storage and spread about the jail for their guests.

But the students arrested at the scene of the riot were never prosecuted. Instead, District Attorney Carol S. Vance singled out Nichols and four other radicals for prosecution, despite the fact that they had not been involved in the riot. During the dormitory melee only two of the five was on the scene— sleeping in their rooms. Nichols and one other were twenty miles away, and a third, Douglas Waller, was already in jail. The so-called "TSU 5" were charged with "assault with intent to murder" one of the policemen injured in the riot. This was under the DA's loose interpretation of an unused 1925 Texas riot law which stipulates that anyone engaged in any phase of a riot is responsible for any offense committed in the riot.

Like his comrades, Nichols was jailed under $10,000 bond. It took him forty-six days to raise bail. By the time he was released in June of 1967, the junior found he had flunked all his courses (ruining his grade-point average) and had been suspended from school. Blacklisted, it was fourteen months before he could land a full-time job hauling garbage out of the posh homes in the River Oaks Property Owners Association to the Sunnyside Dump for $1.65 an hour. Eventually Nichols got a job as a machinist and enrolled as a part-time sophomore at South Texas Junior College to bring his grade-point average back up above the C level.

After being incarcerated, suspended, and blacklisted, it turned out that Nichols was not going to be prosecuted for murder. In October of 1968, the first "TSU 5" case ended in a hung jury and the District Attorney chose not to prosecute Nichols and the other three. In the end, DA Vance charged Nichols and Walker with possession of pistols—punishable by up to two years in jail. (The cases are still pending at this writing.) As Nichols observed in the living room of his frame home, "Being innocent is irrelevant. They can get you without convicting you, without even trying you. They can get you just by pointing the finger at you."

While public officials are perfectly willing to take care of radicals like Nichols, they prefer to see the job done by the educators themselves. It is a faster, cleaner, more effective system that generally does not get caught in the contradictions of the legal system. Politicians arm educators with a host of tough statutes and expect them to be implemented. As Michigan governor William Milliken puts it, "We have the universities for the purposes of education. They are not supposed to be exercises in political democracy."

Lawmakers and regents have seen to it that schools like Berkeley can keep nearly all student and non-student radicals off campus. California's Mulford Act gives campus authorities the power to order non-student undesirables off campus. Each week about half a dozen non-student politicians, pamphleteers, speakers, and panhandlers are quietly "Mulforded" off campus. The law is especially useful for keeping suspended students and "outside agitators" away from Berkeley. Administrators have emergency power to put any violent student, or any student who threatens to be violent, on interim suspension.

But Berkeley and other schools often find their rules are too good. They have an impossible time nabbing everyone they can get. For example, during the February, 1969, Third World strike, the school had to supplement its forty-six-man police force with eight deans and scholarship officers. The deans acted as police spotters, scanning live crowds and thumbing through photographs for the faces of students they knew through their counseling work. The scholarship officers were especially helpful in identifying Third World protestors they had met through their confidential aid work. But as Dean Roland Maples explains, "It was still impossible to identify everyone and it's the kind of thing that will make students shy away from the dean's office for regular counseling. They'll figure being known by the dean is a political liability."

The deans funnel their information to a chief prosecutor who is a seminarian, not a lawyer. Willis A. Shotwell, Berkeley's Coordinator of Facilities and Regulations, taught New Testament studies at a Baptist divinity school for thirteen years before coming to Berkeley. As chief disciplinarian, Shotwell investigates the university's cases against students with the aid of two campus policemen (one is nicknamed "Dean Pig" by the kids). Shotwell serves as a prosecutor before the Committee on Student Conduct, which is composed of seven faculty members and students.

The Berkeley disciplinarian freely admits his job is a tough one. For example, in early 1969, twenty-eight strikers were placed on interim suspension pending the outcome of their disciplinary trials. Obviously this guilty-until-proven-innocent policy is a liability for the student who may be acquitted in a hearing several months later. Therefore the Regents require that interim-suspended students must have their hearings within two weeks. But as it turned out, only four of the twenty-eight interim-suspended strikers had their hearings within two weeks. Legal complications, plus the refusal of city police to hand over their evidence prior to separate civil court action, caused delays. As a result, Shotwell had to "modify the interim suspensions of twenty-four students to let them go to class, the library and health service."

Shotwell contends that his scholarly background makes up for a lack of legal training. "I'm a historian trained in weighing all the evidence, balancing out every side and coming up with conclusions. My first book, *The Biblical Exegisis of Justin Martyr* (which examined the method of biblical exegisis employed by Justin Martyr—first great apologist for the Christian church), didn't get a bad review. Everyone agreed that I knew what I was talking about. On the other hand, I've accumulated some legal knowledge about what the courts say regarding discipline and so forth. This is useful background."

Disciplinary hearings are sometimes complicated by the fact that student defendants bring their own lawyers. In these situations, the university sends its own counsel. But Shotwell points out that the chairman of the judiciary, a law professor, tries to minimize legal incursions. "When the lawyers try to justify their existence by cross-examining, and so forth, the chairman stops them. He'll admonish the lawyers: 'Gentlemen, this is not a legal court, we don't go by adversary procedures. We go our own way. We are concerned with what is best for the university. All we are worried about is whether the defendant did it and what his penalty should be.'"

As a prosecutor Shotwell has an admirable record. In his

first fifty cases only ten ended in acquittal. Nine were suspended or dismissed, and the remainder were put on probation, censured, or given warnings.

One advantage of the university judicial system for Shotwell is that few of his cases are overturned. While the Committee on Student Conduct recommends student penalties, it is Chancellor Roger Heyns who must make final authorization of probation and suspension. Heyns, who has suspended more students than any other college president in the country, doubles as the campus agent for appeals.

From time to time, some people suggest to Shotwell that combined campus-civil prosecution of a student is double jeopardy. But Shotwell, who has abandoned work on his pending book, *The Battles and Battleground of the Maccabees,* to work overtime on discipline, disagrees. "It's just like the army or business. If you commit a crime in the armed services you are responsible under military and common law. If you knock up one of the company secretaries you may lose your job and face a paternity suit too."

Of course some frustrated administrators feel that present campus counter-insurgency tactics don't work. Not long before announcing his own resignation in the summer of 1969, Berkeley's executive vice-chancellor, Earl Cheit, raised the possibility of spraying demonstrators with a "radioactive material" and "then going around later with a geiger counter to discover who the culprits are." But these tactics may be unnecessary. Official stereotyping and repression of radicals has given rise to an ominous new tide of campus vigilantism.

At American University in Washington, D.C., thirty fraternity men forced out a group of twenty-five protestors occupying the campus administration building. Columbia athletes have blocked food from being passed in to students holding Low Library. At Stanford, counterrevolutionaries shouted down radicals protesting war research. Harvard students burned an SDS dummy in effigy. But few of these conservative students have taken their work as seriously as a twenty-one-year-old University of Michigan senior named Leonard Paul Smith. His story shows how innocent students can be victimized by self-styled campus freedom fighters and suggests an ominous first step toward the campus police state.

During the summer of 1968, while officially employed as a nighttime clerk for the FBI in Detroit, Smith tried to carry out an unusually imaginative plan for subverting SDS and student activism in Ann Arbor. His proposed venture was titled "Operation Textbook,"[1] with each phase spelled out in a two-page Xeroxed document on CIA letterhead. In three phases, "Operation Textbook" called for (1) organizing a

[1]CENTRAL INTELLIGENCE AGENCY
Washington, D.C. 20505

SUBJECT: Operation Textbook

PHASE   I:   To initiate, centralize and strengthen a conservative yet politically autonomous student organization. This organization should permeate every facet of the student activist life. The steering committee of the organization may be aware of Government support but this knowledge must not filter down into the main body of the group. Agency money will be used to support this organization. Agency personnel must limit their action to a strictly organizational nature.

PHASE  II:   New Left organizations and student radical groups must be kept in internal disruption from within. Decentralization of these groups is evident and must be encouraged and fostered. This will be accomplished from within by Bureau contacts. The Bureau will be completely responsible for all Phase II projects.

PHASE III:   Actual interruption, destruction and intervention in New Left affairs. This Phase will be accomplished only when Phase I is strongly under way and Phase II is in progress. All Phase III projects will be accomplished solely by Agency supervision.

conservative student alliance to "permeate every facet of the student activist life," with covert Agency support; (2) using FBI contacts to keep "New Left organizations and student radical groups in internal disruption from within"; and (3) the actual "interruption, destruction and intervention in New Left Affairs," under "Agency supervision."

To carry out Phase 1, Smith tried to lure several old friends into collaboration with him by promising free rent and future government jobs. One of his confidants became frightened and exposed the plan to University of Michigan president Robben Fleming. The FBI, fumbling for an explanation, said Smith "was acting on his own." Smith resigned from the FBI. While it appears likely that Smith enjoyed the tacit or direct approval of the FBI on the plot, there is no proof that the CIA was really in on the plan. The "Operation Textbook" document could have been a forgery.

An enigma to his friends, Len's secret passion had always been espionage. He was fascinated with the political applications of fighting crime. "When he talked about communism," says Sue Wilder, a close friend, "you could close your eyes and think you were hearing J. Edgar Hoover himself." In February of 1968, he became a full-time FBI night-shift clerk in Detroit with the hope of attending special agent training school after graduation. The FBI refused to discuss his duties, except to confirm that he was a clerk. The Detroit director Paul Stoddard says, "A clerking experience is like becoming a mason: you learn how to lay the bricks." Apparently a good apprentice, Smith quickly assumed responsibilities that took him outside the office. He carried an unregistered concealed weapon and an official FBI identification packet, which included a government vehicle operator's license.

He also had access to the entire Detroit FBI headquarters

in the Federal Building. A former girlfriend, Chris Frizell, recalls an evening in the spring of 1968 when Smith took her there for a tour. She saw Director Stoddard's office, the well-stocked gun vault, the card files on radicals, even the unlisted eleventh floor of the building where the communications equipment is kept. In the presence of another agent, Jim Sturgis, Smith described an exciting mission earlier that evening when they had stalked a top-ten criminal.

At the end of the summer of 1968, Smith says he landed a big back-to-school assignment, which arrived in an unmarked envelope. A two-page document, on CIA letterhead, spelled out the three-phase "Operation Textbook" plan. He also claims that he received verbal instructions to set up the student alliance. In early August he began telling close friends that he was now "working for the CIA under the FBI cover." This admission was not an indiscretion. Len had made a conscious decision to try to build the conservative student alliance from a base of close friends. Len's roommate, John Bologna, agreed to become codirector of "Operation Textbook" on the promise of free rent and tuition.

"We'll have all the money you want," Len assured his friend, explaining that the subsidies would be funneled through a safe-deposit box at the post office. A few weeks later Len shelled out $400 for initial payment on the apartment.

One evening, Len and his roommate drove downtown to the FBI office and made calls to three other students they hoped would join the battle against SDS and the New Left. Of the three, only one girl expressed lukewarm interest. She was an old girl friend, a brunette named Ellen Heyboer. A German major, she had been spending the summer in Europe. On August 13, the very evening of her return, Len came over to give her the sales pitch and to show her what was by now a three-page document. It consisted of the conservative alliance preamble and the two-page "Operation Textbook" plan on CIA letterhead. Ellen, "in a zombie state" after several sleepless nights of travel, took the document and filed it in a drawer.

Ellen was not especially interested in the alliance to begin with, and after Len gave her the FBI tour complete with a look at the secret FBI rooms and a peek at the files of well-known University of Michigan activists, she was put off by the whole plan. She finally told her fiancé about the scheme and he, in turn, informed the university's assistant director of student organizations. Eventually the story got to President Fleming, who showed an interest in learning more about it. Ellen met Fleming and gave him the documents. Fleming asked Len to stop by his office to chat about the situation. At that point the budding FBI agent realized, he never should have left the documents—if that's what they were—with a partner like Ellen.

Shortly after 9 P.M. on September 25, Ellen heard a knock on her door. Ellen was too scared to answer. A few minutes later the phone rang. It was Len, calling from his apartment. Did she have the documents? No, Fleming had them. Len was furious. "You're in big trouble, El," he said. "This isn't going to end tomorrow, next week, or next month."

Immediately after hanging up, Len notified the FBI in Detroit that the document was out. Then he and a friend burned the remaining evidence. The friend says, "All papers with a CIA letterhead (there were several) were fed to the garbage disposal. Then we drove out of town and burned the remaining papers in an open field." The documents included two copies of the combination number for the rented post-office safe plus confidential reports. The next day Len went to see the Ann Arbor FBI. He also went to see President Fleming to tell him "it was all a joke."

Detroit FBI director Stoddard and Ann Arbor agent Ray Coglin felt obliged to offer Fleming a private explanation of Smith's activities. "They kept repeating that the FBI is 'much too professional' to be involved in these shenanigans," says Fleming. "They maintained that if he did anything like this, he did it strictly on his own." Fleming says he was not convinced.

As a young man planning a career with the FBI, Len was aware of the three-year penalty and $1,000 fine for impersonating a federal officer. But he insisted, "In all my activities, I was acting under orders from the FBI and CIA. That's all I can say." He claims he has no worries about prosecution. "I can't tell all the details. I was in the middle of the thing, but it's obvious that a person in my position was just a small part of the operation. I suppose they chose someone like me because they needed a person who knew the campus and had contacts, not some 30-year-old agent who would be a dead giveaway.

"I understand this is going on at Madison, Berkeley and Columbia, but obviously I don't know for sure. Of course, I do know some details that can't be revealed. The Bureau and the CIA have a lot more power than any writers do because I have nothing to fear if the story gets printed. The FBI knows the whole story right now—and so does the CIA.

"The only thing I regret is that I had to lie afterwards, the hoax bit. No one likes to lie, especially to his friends. But orders are orders. Actually I guess it was a mistake to use my friends in the first place. I shouldn't have gone to them."

He preferred not to dwell on the past, but rather to look

toward the future. "I hope to go back to journalism school and study like I should have done all along. I don't want to get involved with bureau work again. Maybe I can make it in public relations. . . . "

But even if Len Smith had succeeded in crushing SDS and the radical movement in Ann Arbor, he would have solved only one of the problems facing today's colleges. At many schools the student body president has become a bail bonds-man, the student newspaper editor has replaced AP with Liberation News Service, the young professor is exhorting black students to defend themselves with guns, and the campus minister is sheltering local cell meetings.

Against these pernicious forces one university president had only three means of defense: a way with words, his foil, and a high-powered public relations operation. Fortunately, Dr. S. I. (Don) Hayakawa had all three. The well-known semanticist fenced weekly at an athletic club in downtown San Francisco and was carefully groomed by his personal publicist, on loan from his right-wing millionaire friend W. Clement Stone.

On December 2, 1968, his first school day as Acting President of San Francisco State College, Hayakawa wel-comed 600 police onto the campus at 7 A.M. Urging moder-ation with students, he vainly tried to get police to wear floral leis as peace symbols. Later in the morning Haykawa demon-strated his own language and thought in action by charging through a student mob and ripping wires out of a soundtruck. As photographers snapped his picture for front pages across the country, Hayakawa beamed and said "It's the most ex-citing thing since my tenth birthday when I rode a roller coaster for the first time . . ."

During the next two weeks he was engulfed in the politics

of joy. Hayakawa watched appreciatively as the police prodded strikers across the campus commons. Suburban police
departments begged for a chance to send their rookies to the
campus for spring training. But Hayakawa only had eyes for
seasoned regulars. From the window of his office he mar-
veled at the police efficiency. "It was a pleasure to see their
training improve as the days went on." On January 23, when
the police surrounded 459 students attending an "illegal
rally" and arrested them, Hayakawa experienced nirvana.
"It was a perfect police sweep, a complete joy to watch. I'm
sure it will go down in police manuals as a classic maneuver,
a textbook case."

But Hayakawa made sure that the police and students
didn't completely steal the show. He always held major press
conferences on violent days. Then he would retreat to his
office to watch the show on TV while sipping scotch with
colleagues. PR man Harvey Yorke explains, "We usually
found that every minute we could get Don on Cronkite was
one minute less of bloodshed."

By the time the strike ended in March of 1969, Hayakawa
had become a national celebrity. He had visited with President Nixon, spoken before a Congressional Committee, appeared on national television countless times, and joked with
reporters about running for "Emperor of California." At the
University of Colorado he put on his famous tam-o-shanter
and did a dance in rhythm to the derisive chants of dissident
students.

But most of the time Hayakawa was busy courting middle-
class audiences. His so-called tough style was seen during
one of his speaking tours in the late spring of 1969. While
traveling by jet to a meeting in Los Angeles of the Pacific
Coast Electrical Contractors Association, Hayakawa glanced

at a copy of the campus paper, the *Daily Gater*. He had cut off the paper's funds and tried to have it banned for its less than sympathetic coverage of his regime. The paper survived independently through ads and benefits. Turning to public relations aide Harvey Yorke, Hayakawa asked, "Aren't these kids all working in university facilities, can't we throw the little bastards out?" Yorke, a twenty-year veteran of the Air Force, shook his head. "I wouldn't try anything until summer vacation." Hayakawa sputtered, then leaned back in his seat and dozed off.

During the limousine ride from the airport, an electrical-contracting executive asked Hayakawa if the campus activists were being led around by Moscow. Hayakawa denied it. "I resent the notion that outsiders are running this thing. We're quite capable of growing our own sons of bitches right here on campus."

Hayakawa's speech in the Century Plaza Hotel was an overwhelming success. The contractors were so impressed that they gave him a plaid hard-hat, an obvious reference to Hayakawa's symbolic tam-o-shanter. Afterwards, the president took a group of electrical-contracting executives up to his fifteenth floor suite for cocktails and a panoramic view of Beverly Hills. They laughed appreciatively at the inscription on Hayakawa's cigarette lighter, a gift from a Marine regiment in Vietnam, which read "When you've got 'em by the balls, their hearts and minds are soon to follow." During the ensuing conversation Hayakawa spelled out his ideas for campus reorganization. He planned to consolidate academic power in the hands of the central administration and curb the autonomy of social science departments that have led radical causes. Hayakawa also planned to block liberalization of the art department curriculum and discipline campus radicals more effectively. By lowering the student fee allocation from $10 to $1, he had pushed the student government toward bankruptcy. Now the students wouldn't be able to finance their experimental college or tutorial programs. He was also putting pressure on clerical officials to prevent the Ecumenical House from being used as a staging area for the strikers.

While Hayakawa was talking, PR man Yorke called SF State vice-presidents Earl Jones and Frank Dollard[2] and took notes on the results of a student government election. Hayakawa had voided the election in advance. This turned out to be a smart move, because radicals swept all but one student government seat. Students also voted for the immediate ouster of Hayakawa and Air Force ROTC. Yorke passed the bad news to Hayakawa and the president grabbed the phone.

"Is there any evidence of fraud. . . . Well that's o.k. because I already declared the results invalid. . . . No don't wait. Say the election is voided. . . . Well I know the *Berkeley Barb* isn't going to like it, but I guess we're used to that by now. . . . Take a hard line, be real mean and nasty with the students. . . . Use Draconian methods. . . ."

Hayakawa laughed slightly into the phone and then turned to his guests, "They want to know who Draco was."

After Hayakawa hung up, he mentioned that he would accept no speaking engagements during the summer. This would leave him free to work in his college office on plans for the future. Thanks to the strike, Hayakawa's office had all the comforts of home—a big TV, a well-stocked liquor cabinet, and a refrigerator. "I enjoyed myself immensely during all the

---

[2]In the Summer of 1969, Dr. Dollard announced he would resign his vice-presidency and return to teaching.

rioting," he said, beaming. "Whenever there was any trouble, I stocked up for lunch in the office. From then on the biggest problem was whether to have sardines or *pâté de fois gras.*"

# EPILOGUE

by

**Laurence J. Kirshbaum**

Until we began this book last September, I always thought of myself as a detached and dispassionate journalist, digging out all sides of a story. During my college years (1962–66) I worked as a reporter for, then Managing Editor of the *Michigan Daily*. I always preferred the front page with its who-what-where certitudes and 60-point headlines to the ambiguities of the editorial page with Feiffer cartoons and New Left clichés. As a reporter for *Newsweek*, working in Detroit after graduation, I felt completely at home in a sleek, expository medium. I was, after all, the perfect *Newsweek* subscriber—suburban pad, two cars, $17,000 family income, savings account, stock portfolio, American Express card.

This probably explains why the magazine's computer kept sending me special introductory offers. Like many news-magazine readers, I wanted to believe that corporation presidents were men of social vision, that athletes were artists with pigskin and horsehide, that behind every police officer's badge beat the heart of an Eagle Scout. But I, the reader, would often suffer twinges of conflict with me, the reporter, who had seen these superheroes up a little too closely. As a reporter, I had watched with astonishment as four top General Motors executives arrived in Cadillacs for a public ceremony wearing exactly the same navy blue dandruff-flecked suits and dark ties. I had seen Denny McClain butt into a batting-practice line and jab his bat into the ribs of a shortstop who tried to restrain him. I had witnessed the National Guard literally execute several black men who did not stop their station wagon quite fast enough during the Detroit riot.

That last episode was probably the high point for Larry Kirshbaum, dispassionate journalist. On a darkened east side street, the blacks lay on the ground in varying stages of disembowelment, their writhing bodies throwing up specks of vomit and blood into my notebook. I leaned over and captured their words for Page 20:

"Three bloodied Negroes spilled out into the street; a fourth slumped across the back seat. 'There ain't even a goddam penknife in the car,' protested one of the Negroes. Said a guardsman: 'We didn't know that, pal.'"

Not that I was insensitive. It is simply that a journalist does not put down his personal impressions for his New York editors unless he is truly a specialist. Each Monday morning, I would open up the new issue of *Newsweek* and count how many quotes, how many paragraphs, how many lines were the result of my work, so that I could respond properly when friends and relatives would ask, "which are your stories?" I would shuffle through the magazine pointing out the meager results of my handiwork, knowing all the time that the "real" story was rattling around in my subconscious or leaking out in the form of water-cooler anecdotes. The editors had asked me to collect all the "sights, sounds and smells," but somehow the final copy looked and sounded and smelled like New York.

Since my opinions were not sought, except in rare instances, I stopped trying to develop a larger world view. Instead, like many of my colleagues, I relied on an intuitive gut reaction to subjects, evaluating them with my mental shit detector. When Robben Fleming arrived in Ann Arbor to assume the presidency of the University of Michigan, I was flattered that he spent nearly an hour with me, away from a reception in his honor, patiently answering questions by phone that he had obviously been through before (probably with the *Time* reporter). I naturally figured that any president willing to help me make a deadline, by answering questions at 11 P.M., couldn't be all bad. My file to New York was so favorable that a colleague chided me the next day about working for the alumni association.

I reacted to radical students less favorably. At best, I would come away from interviews with snatches of platitudinous harangues etched into my notebook and the unanswered question still in my mind "But what are they really angry about?" I just couldn't accept their unchecked alienation. When I got back to the office, I realized they had often been putting me on, a fact that provided a rationale for dealing harshly with them in my files. I have always felt ambivalent about radicals, sympathetic to some of their objectives, but hung-up on their peculiar habits. To be sure, when I was at

college, I recognized their importance to a budding journalist. I worked at the *Michigan Daily,* I knew a lot of radicals
who hung out there, but I still wanted to disassociate my
self-image from them. My life-style was somewhat radical,
since I would stay up a lot of nights, sleep a lot of days, hate
class, and wear unwashed clothes. But I still prided myself
on being a fraternity man. Friends in the house would kid
me by saying sarcastically, "You're real normal, Lar," which
always bothered the hell out of me because I really wanted
to be normal in their terms. That is why I would doggedly go
to the Undergraduate Library on Sundays, when the *Daily*
was not in operation, so that my fraternity and sorority friends
would look over and say to themselves, "that Kirshbaum
may work with those freaks at the *Daily,* but inside he's just
like us."

When I became Managing Editor of the *Daily,* I was determined to cut down the paper's heavy coverage of the New
Left. I pulled off my first coup in March, 1965, on the night
of the world's first teach-in. While students rallied on the
snow-covered "Diag" and discussed the issues all night in
lecture halls and classrooms, I was cloistered in the *Daily*
building, playing omniscient editor. I toned down a reporter's
enthusiastic teach-in story and buried it under a small head-
line. I told myself that I was acting journalistically by not
getting carried away with these antiwar shenanigans. Later,
after the presses rolled at 2 A.M., I walked over to Angell
Hall and realized I had been wrong about my own feelings.
Thousands of students were divided into auditoriums and
rooms, arguing excitedly about the Vietnam war. They were
disappointed by the small story and I had to go on pretending
that my editing had been correct.

I was not to have that feeling of "where-the-hell-have-I-been?" until October of 1968. By then, I had graduated, served with *Newsweek* in Detroit and San Francisco, and then been granted a leave to research and write this book.

My first destination was Madison, the home of the University of Wisconsin. I felt strangely underweight. No notebook, no camera, no editor's query on my person. I felt like a student rather than a reporter, especially since I was scheduled to live in a freshman dormitory. The Madison dorm offered the same kind of revelation as walking over to Angell Hall. During my freshman year at Ann Arbor, most of my spare time had been taken up with horseplay or fraternity pledge meetings. But these Wisconsin freshmen wore a very grim look. Anti-draft literature was passed out at the dining hall entrance; small SDS caucuses flourished in the snack bar; many of the black students kept strictly to themselves as if they didn't want to acquire "honkie" habits by association. Nowhere was the rebellious spirit more evident than in the TV room.

One night, shortly before the presidential election, the hour changed and a special program on Nixon and Humphrey began. The crowd, which had been enthusiastically watching a western, hooted at this one kid, the channel adjuster, to change stations. I remember my freshman year, frantically soaking up the latest reports on the Cuban missile crisis; and my sophomore year, sitting in the fraternity chapter room, with tears streaming from my eyes, as they laid John Kennedy to rest; and my junior year when I avidly followed the campaign speeches of Johnson and Goldwater. But these freshmen were very cynical after a year marred by the assassinations of Martin Luther King and Bobby Kennedy, not to mention the debacle at the Chicago convention. Thereafter, I was to notice that, no matter what campus or what kind of group, whenever Richard Nixon appeared on television or in a news clip, made a speech, or whatever, he would be greeted with the enthusiasm reserved for detergent commercials.

This cynicism extended to the classroom. I sat in on an introductory anthropology recitation, a small class of fifteen, in which the young teacher was trying to elicit responses on the subject of "Man and Society," a topic he thought would appeal to them. It was shortly before a test, and the teacher kept hinting that if they didn't pay attention they would miss important material. In my freshman year, I was frantic if I missed a single pearly word of instruction before a test. But this class hardly seemed to be paying attention. One girl was drawing trees, others were passing notes. Finally, the anxious instructor asked a student in the third row, who happened to be reading an underground newspaper, why he wasn't paying attention. The kid looked up as though he had just been asked to produce his draft card and remarked that the class was a "drag." All of a sudden, like a volcano, the whole class erupted in laughter—not laughter at a classmate who made a mistake, but a unified taunt at the instructor for asking such a stupid question in such a stupid class. It was as if they had all stood up and said simultaneously, "fuck you, buddy, you take care of your business and we'll take care of ours."

The instructor, a young fellow struggling along that dusty road to a Ph.D., was obviously taken back. I could see the wheels turning, as he thought to himself, "I've been at this grind for nine years without complaints and here are these young punks in their second month of classes and already they're a bunch of smart–asses." But he was scared, too, because he was seeing what his young students really thought of his sheepskin, his credentials, and his beloved anthropology.

I spent a lot of time with these freshmen at Wisconsin and I kept getting the same eerie feeling that they had underground television piped into their rooms. I realized this is precisely what adults believe today; that somewhere, in a pot-filled basement, sits a communist-financed guru from Cuba, who is disseminating hate messages in little beeps like a Clorets commercial. Many of the freshmen were confused; they were hung-up on radical tactics, a subject getting much attention as SDS planned its election protest.

After one meeting, an obviously troubled freshman was accosted by a senior radical leader. There ensued the usual argument that SDS members have become accustomed to, the "I agree with you—but why must you be so violent" reproach. The senior, a cherubic-faced boy with ringlets of hair dancing on his scalp, kept parrying the freshman's thrusts with patented Marcusean arguments on how violence on campus must be considered in the context of violence in Vietnam. Finally, the freshman played what he thought was his trump card. He asked how the movement could avocate free speech and still hoot down speakers they disagreed with. The senior, who was active in the history student fight discussed in Chapter 3, smiled and shrugged. "Look. The Dow Jones Corporation can publish the *Wall Street Journal* to discuss its viewpoint. The New York Times Corporation can print the *New York Times*. And I am allowed to put out the History Student Association newsletter. That is what you call free speech in America."

It wasn't so much the argument, as the tone, that was so convincing. The senior, with his wry smile and cascading locks and dirty sweater, had, by the merest inflection, conjured up the big establishment beast, the *Times,* and then ever so gently, introduced the mouse against this monster. His was the voice of the tailor showing his threadbare coat and beseeching a purchase. The freshman bought it. After spewing forth questions for forty-five minutes, he just stopped and nodded. Then he put his arm up on the senior's shoulder for a moment and walked away. I could see him leaving the building, walking down the hill in the cool night illuminated by the white spectre of the capitol in the background. His mind throbbing, his lips perhaps repeating the senior's argument which he in turn would use on a skeptical roommate, a girlfriend, or parent who might say to him, "Yes, yes, but what about violence? . . ." Perhaps the highest compliment to the success of radicals has been their ability to build a free-wheeling culture within the tight university structure.

The radicals have succeeded in building their movement under the noses of the very adults who design the buildings, shape the curriculum, pick the teachers, assign roommates, hover over off-campus life. Not to mention the tactical support given institutions like football which emphasize "fair play" under the watchful eye of adult referees. And what do the students have to work with? Not their rooms, which are subject to invasion by "resident advisors." Not their student governments, which are routed by administrators as soon as money for the band is turned over to ghetto tutorials. Not even their vacations, which are taken up with recuperation and begging dad for enough money to pay for the next term.

What the students do have is an invisible culture which draws its *raison d'être* from the antics of adults. The radicals can easily convert a regular ceremonial event into a piece of guerilla theater, by simply allowing the administrators, faculty, and politicians, to be the lead actors.

I can recall a ROTC ceremony at Cornell this past May which the radicals turned into a charade, by passing out pictures of napalmed babies at the door and cheering at the wrong time. Suddenly, the young soldiers, stomping amateurishly in cadence around a large gymnasium, looked like a poor man's marching band. Especially funny was the sight of President James Perkins, winking at familiar faces and trying to appear at ease, his large belly protruding in contrast to those of the ramrod-straight colonels who were marching him around the floor before several thousand uneasy students. When the band played the "Star Spangled Banner," there was a long, painful moment as nearly everyone hesitated before rising. This patriotic ritual had taken on an element of shame. The climactic moment, however, occurred when the local chairman of the Daughters of the American Revolution, built like Charles de Gaulle, her skirt billowing to her calves, strode from the reviewing stand to bestow an award upon some lucky cadet. The crowd issued a very loud mock cheer. Afterward, I saw many ROTC graduates picking up copies of the SDS brochure as they walked out on their way home. After two years worth of military drilling, their morale had been damaged in one short ceremony.

But the damage to our armed forces was not nearly as interesting to me as the reaction of university officials. In their judgment, naturally, the ROTC ceremony was a success because it went off as planned without disruption. I was sitting in President Perkins' office a few days later, as he described the week's events to his board chairman, Bob Purcell, who was calling from a vacation retreat. Perkins put his feet up on a side table and gave the following nonstop briefing:

"Hello, Bob, let me give you the rundown. SDS was planning to sit in today, but the radical professor Dowd read them the riot act last night, so I haven't heard hide or hair of them. . . . Of course you remember it was precisely after such a meeting at Harvard that a small minority took the administration building. . . . We're also working on the black studies crisis. Our boy Turner, you know, the new chairman, wants to make an appointment that is highly unacceptable to me, so we're still working on that one. . . . And finally, Barton Hall, the moderate group, is continuing to meet. As you know, SDS is vehemently against the Barton Hall effort, which I feel is a very good reason for me to support it."

These same war games pervaded the "crisis" at Cornell. At one point, a lower-echelon administrator tried desperately to locate his boss, a top vice-president, in order to resolve some student issue. But he couldn't find any of the top administrators in their offices. After a good deal of sleuthing, all he could get was a "special" phone number—a hot line— where all the key administrators could be reached in an extreme, extreme emergency.

The role of fright was emphatically brought home to me when I got to Harvard after the big bust there. One afternoon I went to see Talcott Parsons, the man who made sociology a respectable discipline at a time when most "sociologists" were still drawing concentric circles on urban grids. As a pioneer, Parsons could be expected to embrace the black studies developments, which might well open up a new dimension to social science. But Parsons, by now a paunchy, washed-out looking man, sat in his office and pounded on his chair as he described the threat black studies poses for Harvard. "If we got a man like Eldridge Cleaver," he stormed, "it might mean 300 years of hard intellectual labor down the drain. I'm not going [pound] to let that [pound] happen." A few hours later, I was sitting in the office of Robert McCloskey, the government chairman and an active member of the "conservative" faculty caucus. He received a call from a colleague who was on his way to Cornell to talk his daughter out of becoming involved in the moderate Barton Hall movement. The colleague feared that the black students would try to "get revenge" if she became too identified with the opposition. There sat McCloskey, a man himself passionately involved in the affairs of his university, wholeheartedly in sympathy with this colleague, who was reacting hysterically to the pictures of guns which had appeared in the *New York Times* and elsewhere. At no point had the blacks ever made any threats. In fact, they armed themselves only because of rumors that whites were going to storm their Bastille. But in the mind of a hysterical professor, 300 miles away, his daughter's life was in imminent danger.

It was impossible for me to understand how these men, living in such close proximity to students, could be so completely wrapped up in their own emotional cocoons that they had no idea of what it means to be a radical.

In a way, however, I had been getting a firsthand lesson in the difficulty of direct communication through my changing relationship with my parents. I am not going to give you the conventional generation gap portrait. My parents ably survived the early-teen pimple crisis, the eighteen-year-old whoring crisis, and finally the twenty-two-year-old identity crisis. With great relief they saw me married and employed under respectable conditions. The kinds of family-shattering issues, such as drugs and premarital cohabitation, never fissured our relationship. We had, to use my father's favorite expression, "good communication," but it was a communication more of the intellect than the viscera, as I was to discover during the course of writing this book.

Naturally, when they knew their son was writing a book on "Student Power," they became as interested in the subject as though they were the parents of a college-bound freshman. It was an intellectual challenge to help me find "new slants." My father, a financial consultant, based in Chicago but spending a good deal of time in New York, would try to get a "feel" of public attitudes by talking to elevator operators or taxi drivers, while my mother would eagerly send me press clippings in San Francisco.

Periodically my travels took me through Chicago where my parents questioned me about "student power" the way thousands of parents no doubt debriefed their children back from battlefields at Cambridge and Berkeley. Our first session occurred after my two-week stay at Madison, where I had seen the radicalization process described earlier. My father, consulting his taxi-driver oracles, said "everybody wanted to know" how many students were "radical"—2%, 5%, 10%. I said that his numbers were both understated and irrelevant, like asking how many people at the Chicago Board of Trade support the capitalist system. I tried to explain that all students at prestigious schools agree that major changes are necessary. The only issue is one of timing and tactics.

During these discussions with my father, the real question in my mind was, how many students make up the non-radical campus fringe which is still under the control of the Boy Scouts, the ROTC, and the DAR. Somehow I couldn't get my father, an intelligent man, to shake off his preconceptions. I would go to Alabama and report how black students were trying to crack "Bear" Bryant's football team, or Texas where even the flutteriest Longhorn belle was "uneasy" over the once and future presence of Lyndon B. Johnson, war hawk. But my father, living in the day-to-day turmoil of the stock market rather than that of campus protest, was of course getting a different slant. One time he recommended that I go see the local director of the FBI (which I had already done in Detroit to little avail). At another point, he sounded like a New York taxi driver himself, when he suggested a title for the book—*Has Youth Gone Crazy?*

Since my patience and logic were running thin, I called Herbert Marcuse in from the bullpen and deposited his *One Dimensional Man* on my father's nightstand. He apparently was tremendously impressed, devoured Herbert in about three sittings, and then proceeded to rattle off thoughts about Repressive Desublimation which awed me into exercising the better part of valor, and my constitutional liberties, by remaining silent. After all, if my father had only taken Herbert into his brain, I still had him in my guts. The next day my father went back to the New York Stock Exchange and I returned to Harvard. Sure enough, a few weeks later, when we were both in New York, he was throwing out the same old "what-everybody-wants-to-know" questions, with the latest twist being that his oracles (now more the natty, gray-flannel types) wondered "What could the establishment do to solve student power?"

I guess it was the word "solve" that really got me, because it was an expression I had heard from adults throughout my travels. In their eyes, radicalism is a new kind of riddle for problem solvers, particularly those accustomed to "complexities" in their daily dealings. Like my father, professional men, inside and outside the academies, feel that their experiences in writing New Deal legislation or refinancing railroads can be of great value. One law student at Harvard experienced this attitude when he complained to a professor about the competitive atmosphere, after being kept up all night by the clattering of typewriters in other rooms. The professor sympathetically suggested that the student jot down his "recommendations" and "leave them under my door." To my father, "student power" was, like Repressive Desublimation, an issue not within the realm of his normal life. It was as though we were arguing about whether the Chicago White Sox would finish under .500. I don't think he honestly saw, or deeply felt, the fact that, when we were discussing radicalism, we were also discussing me, a person, trying to sort out his life.

Finally, in one last effort, I really let him have it. One night we were having a late dinner together in New York, with a few drinks, and after gorging ourselves on $7 sirloin and onion rings, I really laid out the dessert. I don't remember the exact thread of the argument, but I do remember saying about twenty-three times that "everything is fucked up"— everything being me, the capitalist system, him, his life, the way he brought me up, the fact that I was there "honked" on $7 steaks and needing his money to raise a family. It was hard to keep my father's attention because he was on the verge of closing a business deal and kept hopping up and down to make phone calls. Each time he came back to the table, I would start up again and he would try to interrupt. "Surely the generation gap isn't so wide that . . ." or "Well, just to get the communication straight . . ." Not to be deterred, I continued talking, or rather shouting. Finally, I rounded off with a flourish. "You just want to analyze the situation, you don't want to understand it." And, with that, I said good-bye and walked out. (I presume he picked up the tab). But I was wrong, because in his own way he really did want to understand. We didn't talk to each other until the next night, just before I was catching a plane out of New York, when we spoke on the telephone.

He simply said to me, "You're a very mature young man," and then we clicked off. At first, I felt as though I had been bribed with some kind of half-hearted compliment, but later I realized he had said what he did because there was nothing else to say. He would have to spend a lot more time thinking about it.

This whole series of episodes took place over an eight-month period, from October to May, so it was natural that I plugged them into my own reporting during that time. I suppose this is some kind of supreme ego, but I honestly feel that my own case is in some ways a miniaturization of what is happening throughout society. On the one hand, there are people like me, in high school, college, the "professional" world, trying to put it all togther, and looking at adults as the prism through which we could dissect the various components. On the other hand, there are fathers, personnel directors, and a lot of administrators, who are trying in their own perverse way to make sense out of what has happened —whether, in fact, youth has gone crazy. Like my father, they can read Marcuse, they can recite the arguments, they can deplore the Vietnam war, or oppose ABM, or support Gene McCarthy. But they won't let themselves feel the real hate, because they've poured their best years into raising this generation and they won't admit that their molds no longer work.

But whether they like it or not, society is going to change, the university is going to change—with very little concern for their wishes. Perhaps President Nixon, who visits such typical campuses as the Air Force Academy and General Beadle State College, doesn't know that he is considered in the same category as a detergent commercial at Berkeley, Wisconsin, or Harvard. But parents everywhere must be feeling the ground swell in their own homes, in their own children.

"Student power" is not a phenomenon, nor a puzzle, but a genuinely violent reaction to adult institutions. That's why, when older people ask me in anguished tones "what should we do?", I can't lay out steps number one, two, three, four. I, for one, am not giving any advice because I'm trying to figure out what I can do. When I came back home in late May to finish this book, I resigned from *Newsweek*. I called the personnel director, a good friend named Rod Gander, to try to offer an explanation for my sudden resignation. He answered, "I know Oz [Editor Osborn Elliott] will want to know, what can *Newsweek* do to keep young people?" It was the proverbial what-everybody-wants-to-know question, for which I have no simple answer. If we had been in the same city, we might have gone out to a restaurant for a $7 steak.

# About the Authors

ROGER RAPOPORT, twenty-three, was born in Detroit and grew up in Michigan. He attended the University of Michigan, where he was editor of the *Michigan Daily,* and graduated in 1968. His articles have appeared in *Esquire, Look, West, Harper's, The Atlantic* and *The Wall Street Journal.* He lives in San Francisco.

LAURENCE J. KIRSHBAUM, twenty-five, was born and raised in Chicago. He attended the University of Michigan, where he was managing editor of the *Michigan Daily,* and graduated in 1966. He worked for two years as a reporter for *Newsweek* magazine in Detroit and San Fransico. He is currently a free-lance writer living in San Francisco with his wife, Barbara.